PRACTICAL MANAGEMENT FOR PRODUCTIVITY

PRACTICAL MANAGEMENT FOR PRODUCTIVITY

John R. Hinrichs, Ph.D.

Management Decision Systems, Inc.
Darien, Connecticut

Van Nostrand Reinhold/Work in America Institute Series

VAN NOSTRAND REINHOLD COMPANY

NEW YORK   CINCINNATI   ATLANTA   DALLAS   SAN FRANCISCO
LONDON   TORONTO   MELBOURNE

Van Nostrand Reinhold Company Regional Offices:
New York   Cincinnati   Atlanta   Dallas   San Francisco

Van Nostrand Reinhold Company International Offices:
London   Toronto   Melbourne

Copyright © 1978 by Litton Educational Publishing, Inc.

Library of Congress Catalog Card Number: 78-9797
ISBN: 0-442-20370-5

Manufactured in the United States of America

Published by Van Nostrand Reinhold Company
135 West 50th Street, New York, N.Y. 10020

Published simultaneously in Canada by Van Nostrand Reinhold Ltd.

15 14 13 12 11 10 9 8 7 6 5 4 3 2 1

Library of Congress Cataloging in Publication Data

Hinrichs, John R.
    Practical management for productivity.

    Includes index.
    1. Labor productivity.   I. Title.
HD57.H5   658.31'42   78-9797
ISBN 0-442-20370-5

This book is dedicated to the hundreds of thousands of workers in the twelve organizations mentioned herein who are able and anxious to contribute in a meaningful way to the productivity and quality of work life in their organizations, and thereby to the health of the American economy. May the system permit them to do so.

VNR/WORK IN AMERICA INSTITUTE SERIES

The VNR/Work in America Institute Series is designed to provide practical insight into new and better ways to advance productivity and the quality of working life. The objective is to create heightened awareness of the opportunities for an enriched work life that can exist in innovative organizations, and to reveal the benefits of linking people and production in a common goal, through clearer understanding of the key factors contributing to worker output and job satisfaction.

The Series will provide guidance on a number of concerns that influence work performance, not only in today's work environment, but also in the even more complex world of work that lies ahead. Titles in the World of Work Series will focus on five fundamental issues affecting the work community: (1) *The quality of working life*, exploring opportunity, recognition, participation, and rewards for employees to optimize their involvement in and contribution to the work organization; (2) *Productivity*, focusing on the human factors in the productivity equation, to increase both individual and organizational output through more effective use of human resources; (3) *Education and the world of work*, discussing ways to improve the match between the entry-level worker and the job, by building bridges from education to the world of work; (4) *Employee-management cooperation*, recognizing that employees contribute important know-how and ingenuity to increase output, reduce waste, maintain product quality, and improve morale; and (5) *National labor force policy*, examining policies of the United States and other industrialized nations as they affect productivity and the quality of working life.

Foreword

An ancient parable—attributed by some to the Chinese—tells of the proper way to drive a tunnel through a mountain. The workers are divided into two groups, which begin to dig from opposite sides of the mountain. When they meet, the tunnel is complete. However, if they do not meet somewhere under the mountain, then the result is not one but two tunnels.

So it is with the contemporary drive to achieve higher productivity in the workplace. One approach strives to achieve greater production, the other reduced labor content. Yet, in the final analysis, the objectives in each instance are identical: to generate ever-higher levels of production—services or goods—for a given level of human effort. But just as it is for the tunnel-drivers of the parable, the great danger exists that somewhere, in the midst of attempts to solve the problem, a common solution will not be reached.

The analogy, of course, is imperfect. Yet, there is an important lesson for today's managers to learn from this bit of ancient wisdom. In the context of finding answers to the nation's intensifying productivity problem, we can ill afford "solutions" that are wasteful of resources, whether human or financial. Enhanced production achieved at the expense of the human factor is ultimately self-defeating; similarly, blind concern for the quality of working life without concomitant concern for production eventually will destroy the very system that created mechanisms for dealing with quality of working-life issues in the first place.

Striking the proper balance between these seemingly opposed viewpoints—like the challenge of driving but one straight and true tunnel—ultimately reduces itself to questions of planning, adaptation, and flexibility. Dr. Hinrichs' analysis of these three factors—based on 12 case studies of experiments to enhance human resource productivity—emphasizes the way in which they can and are being combined by the imaginative organization to make work life more satisfying and rewarding for employees, while at the same time improving productivity.

In commissioning this study, the Work in America Institute's objective was to make a significant contribution to the work community: first, by recognizing the contributions of those innovative organizations that are in the forefront of the movement toward enhanced human resource productivity, and, second, by setting a target and providing a workable methodology for those organizations that have not yet recognized or acted upon this need. We acknowledge with gratitude the financial support of the National Center for Productivity and Quality of Working Life which made possible the research on which this book was based.

JEROME M. ROSOW
President
Work in America Institute, Inc.

Preface

As we approach the decade of the eighties in the United States, it is becoming more and more clear that the productivity of the various organizations and institutions of our society is a national concern.

Problems of inflation, the energy crisis, and an adverse balance of payments which never seem to go away, highlight the dependence of our society on high levels of productivity and productivity growth for maintaining economic health. These broad-scale factors, in conjunction with increasing domestic and foreign competition, and a relative plateau in the productivity increases to be gained from new technology or capital investments, contribute to this concern over productivity.

The problem is highlighted by the statistics. In the United States, output per man-hour dropped 2.7 percent in 1974, the first full year of decline since 1947 and a signal that the issue of productivity warrants the level of concern which it is beginning to receive. In business and commerce, it is being increasingly recognized by management, by government, and by labor that productivity has been a key to our American standard of living and that steps must be taken to enhance it.

In the face of this concern, it is interesting that there is no universally accepted definition of just what productivity is. That is, there is no single set of measures or indicators which a business or government agency can use to measure its productivity. Different measures are used in different situations.

However, there is rather clear acceptance of the fact that productivity should be thought of as a ratio concept—the ratio of the output of goods and services produced or generated by an organization divided by the input used to produce them. Thus, to influence this ratio, one may either try directly to increase the outputs or to reduce the level of inputs into the system.

Efforts to increase productivity in the past have focused largely on technology and capital. They have included attempts to reduce the input costs of production and capital requirements through various labor-saving devices. With the escalating cost of labor and pervasive inflation, and with growing concern about maintaining full employment in the society, there is less political and social leverage in this area than in former years. Similarly, past productivity improvement efforts have also focused on increasing the output of production through more efficient production methods, mechanization, better flow of work, and more efficient management. While there is still considerable room for productivity returns from the introduction of more efficient methods and technology into the production process, the rate of return is probably not as great as it was some years ago when, for example, the assembly line concept revolutionized many manufacturing processes.

A major input to the productivity ratio is the whole area of utilization of human resources. Historically, efforts to improve human resource productivity have focused on asking for "more." Employees have been pressured to work harder and increase their output. In recent years, however, the potential for gains from this strategy has been blunted by legislation, unions, and social norms which no longer permit the "sweatshop" mentality in our business and commercial institutions. As a result, most efforts to increase human resource productivity have come to focus more on the inputs: cutting back staffing levels as much as possible; replacing people by less expensive equipment; and so forth. People are seen as a direct expense, and productivity can be achieved by cutting this expense as much as possible.

Inevitably, this strategy has led to employee resentment and resistance. The result has been a rather pervasive tendency for slowdown. The "rate buster" is universally resented by most workers, not just in union shops. Unions and workers are concerned about spreading the work, and they resist managements' efforts to cut back.

However, many enlightened organizations are beginning to recognize a relatively new area for increasing the productivity of the human resource without reducing the inputs. They are finding that by designing systems which lead to greater employee outputs that are not keyed to the necessity of working harder, they are overcoming the resistance and the restrictions engendered by former efforts to increase human resource productivity. In effect, they are starting to put into practice the old adage "work smarter, not harder." This seems to be the dawning of a new era of enlightened human resource management, with significant implications for enhancing the productivity of many of the institutions of our economy.

This new focus on increasing the output from better human resource management has moved forward on a number of fronts:

1) Concepts of more effective design of jobs have been rather widely adopted. There is growing concern in many organizations with ensuring that individual jobs fully use the skills of the incumbents and then are integrated into total clusters of jobs or project teams so that the right skill levels are combined to achieve production objectives. Job design concepts focus on the skills of the individual, but also on the total team or project group to assure the balanced use of the organization's human resource. We are seeing such strategies in areas such as matrix organizations in product development, team organizations in manufacturing, and even team forms of shared responsibility in the executive suite. The approach capitalizes upon and maximizes the strong points of the individual and builds on the synergy of the group. By-products from effective job design, in addition to optimum skill utilization, include increased job challenge, more involvement in the work, and heightened motivation and commitment for effective performance—which lead to increased productivity.

2) There is growing attention to the effective use of incentives and feedback to increase productivity. It has become increasingly recognized how important it is for workers to experience the achievement of meaningful goals in order to sustain motivation and productivity. Goal setting as a process is being extended further and further in many organizations, with impressive results. Whereas only a few years ago it was primarily thought of in terms of setting objectives for managers and executives through Management by Objectives Programs, more and more the goal-setting process is being applied at all levels. Setting clear performance goals clarifies for the individual

what is expected and provides a frame of reference which is essential for enhancing work motivation. Tied to the goal-setting process are more systematic procedures for providing knowledge of results to the individual. Such knowledge is essential for self-motivation and a base for modifying performance goals to fit the realities of results achieved. In addition, more and more organizations are systematically designing the process of reinforcing the achievement of desired goals. This is accomplished through new approaches toward financial incentive programs, plus various intangible reinforcements such as praise and recognition. The whole goal-setting, feedback, and reinforcement process is being applied in a more consistent and programmed fashion in many organizations, often with dramatic implications for improved productivity.

3) The third focus in attempting to improve human resource productivity has entailed an approach or philosophy which might broadly be characterized under the term "participative management." The thrust of participative management requires the recognition that: most employees are responsible; most employees react positively to an opportunity to have some degree of voice in their own destiny; enlightened management should treat employees as mature adults rather than as dependent children; the health and success of the enterprise is not a unilateral management concern and employees are capable of being involved and caring and contributing; it is possible to institute management approaches which build employee involvement and shared objectives. This approach is an entirely different way of thinking about the employee/management relationship from the traditional viewpoint which looked upon labor as an input to the productive system which could be manipulated passively—increased, decreased, reassigned—in whatever way management desired. Participative management finds its expression in patterns of supervisory style which regularly solicit employee opinions and suggestions, in programs which allow more employee discretion about their working lives such as flexible working hours, and in systematic efforts to enhance cooperation between unions and management to achieve shared objectives. In this area, as well, many organizations are finding substantial productivity payoffs from the human resource.

During the 1950s and 1960s there was a great deal of experimentation in these areas. Concepts of job design blossomed and were widely applied in the somewhat faddish adoption of job enrichment principles. Other experiments extended job enrichment concepts to broader systems and refined the knowledge of how to maximize the use of teamwork and optimize the use of skills. Experimentation with various aspects of participative management and employee involvement added to the store of knowledge on how to implement these concepts. There has also been growing experimentation in the area of goal setting, feedback, and systematic reinforcement to enhance productivity.

Now, in the late 1970s, the insights derived from this early experimentation are being applied more consistently in many organizations, with dramatic results at times. Productivity improvements have been registered in terms of:

1. Increased production—quantity, product quality, reduced costs, decreased scrap, etc.
2. Reduced personnel withdrawal—turnover, absenteeism, tardiness.
3. Reduced organizational disruptions—accidents, strikes, slowdowns, grievances, sabotage, etc.

As a bonus, by implementing some of these strategies for enhancing human resource productivity, many organizations have found that the quality of working life has improved. Quality of working life (QWL) is a force which is increasingly being pushed for within the American economy, as in Europe, by employees, by unions, and by government, as well as by many managements themselves. More and more it is being recognized that QWL and productivity can go together and that an organization does not have to give up productivity in order to make work more satisfying and rewarding for employees. There is a growing technology and interest in achieving QWL, while at the same time enhancing productivity.

This book is an exploration into some of these concepts. A number of experiments in productivity enhancement through more effective utilization of the human resource, which have been undertaken in the United States since 1970, are examined in depth. Then, an attempt is made to synthesize from these experiments the major components of a successful program to enhance human resource productivity and QWL.

This book was commissioned by the Work in America Institute, Inc., through a project funded by the National Center for Productivity and Quality of Working Life in Washington, D.C. Special appreciation is due to Dr. BenAmi Blau, Vice President, Technical Assistance, of the Work in America Institute for initiating the project. The efforts of Mrs. Virginia Lentini in typing and retyping the manuscript were invaluable. In addition, the cooperation of all the personnel who supported the project in the organizations described in the book's case studies is appreciated. Their willingness to innovate and test new programs, structures, and techniques to enhance human resource productivity and, even more, to share their findings and insights with readers of this book—is truly appreciated.

Contents

Foreword / **vii**

Preface / **ix**

1 Introduction / **1**

2 A Poker Game Incentive for Attendance / **9**

3 Enhancing Product Quality / **18**

4 Positive Reinforcement to Enhance Performance / **31**

5 Extending Research Findings from the Psychological Laboratory to the Field Setting / **41**

Interim Summary for Chapters 2–5 Illustrating Behavioral Change Efforts / **65**

6 Building a Participative Management System to Enhance Product Quality / **67**

7 A Participatively Designed Pay Plan / **77**

8 Turning Around a History of Labor/Management Conflict / **88**

9 Transplanting an Open System of Management from One Organization to Another / **103**

Interim Summary for Chapters 6–9 Illustrating Humanistic Change Efforts / **115**

10 Flexible Working Hours to Enhance Productivity and Employee Morale / **118**

11 Innovations to Enhance Productivity in Large-Scale Technology Projects / **137**

12 Job Enrichment in a Large Clerical Organization / **146**

13 Orthodox Job Enrichment for Changing a Management System / **154**

Interim Summary for Chapters 10–13 Illustrating Structural Change Efforts / **169**

14 Conclusion / **171**

Appendix / **185**

Index / **189**

1
Introduction

In 1977, a review of the technical and professional literature dealing with productivity experiments published between 1971 and 1975 was published by the Work in America Institute in Scarsdale, New York. That review—*A Guide to Worker Productivity Experiments in the United States, 1971-75* by Raymond A. Katzell, Penney Bienstock, and Paul H. Faerstein—found 103 studies carried out in the United States during the five year period which dealt with some aspect of worker productivity. This book has been written to amplify on the review. In the literature review, productivity was liberally defined to include factors related to workers' inputs, such as costs, turnover, accidents, or absenteeism, as well as factors related to worker outputs, such as quantity, quality, or value. The study searched eleven major journals for the five year period. It also covered a significantly wider range of publications in the United States and overseas by searching literature abstracts related to psychology, sociology, and personnel management.

To be included in the review, a study had to consist of an experiment of some type in which changes were made in a permanent organization (not in a laboratory setting) with sufficient rigor to follow up on the results and assess changes. The study had to deal with some aspect of productivity and had to treat the changes in a quantitative fashion, rather than solely dealing with impressions or anecdotes.

Our purpose in writing this book was to pick twelve to fifteen of these studies which covered a variety of organizations and productivity experiments and to amplify upon them in nontechnical terms. We wanted to make the often technical and sometimes esoteric descriptions of the programs in the journal articles "come alive" for department managers in organizations. By doing this, we hoped to demonstrate the potential for achieving increased productivity at the departmental level and thus to seed a motivation for experimentation and change among our readers.

From the 103 studies, we picked twenty-one experiments which covered a spectrum of industries and productivity programs. Five of these experiments took place in a single company, so we were, in effect, covering seventeen organizations, which we thought gave a comfortable margin for dropout as we settled on the twelve to fifteen cases for this book. The twenty-one studies picked were the most clear and dramatic demonstrations of the potential for increasing productivity through better human resource management which had been published during the five years of the review. Most of the other studies were excluded because they were redundant, the changes were not very clear, or the results of the experiment were negative.

Eight of the seventeen companies we contacted refused to participate or did not respond to our inquiry. (Four of the companies explicitly said "No" and did not want to publicize their activities and four companies did not reply to our inquiry.) For one other case, it became clear as we pursued it that the actual productivity results were much more ambiguous than the published results, so we decided to exclude this organization as well. Thus, we ended up with eight organizations willing to let us amplify their experiments as cases in this book.

Through discussions with colleagues concerned with the broad area of human resource utilization and quality of working life (QWL), it became evident that many good examples of experimental changes in American industry and business do not find their way into the published literature and thus were not included in the 1971–1975 literature search. The reasons vary: the organization may be too busy innovating to take time to publish the results; the experiment may still be in process and not at a point at which the organization feels that it can be shared; the project may be carried out by line personnel who are not motivated to publish the results as are academic personnel; or (a very prevalent reason) management may not want to disclose information about the experiment either for fear of disrupting it through premature attention or of disclosing for competitors the extent to which they are achieving productivity gains through new forms of organization. However, after contacting a number of organizations, we were able to locate four additional companies which had carried out or were in the process of carrying out significant but unpublished productivity experiments, with measurable results. We have included these four in the casebook.

Each one of our sample of twelve organizations was contacted and visited for a period of one to two days. From the visits, we tried to obtain as broad a perspective as possible and to consult with various source persons. In addition to the individual responsible for the experiment, we tried to talk with senior management, department managers, union representatives, and employees. This was not always possible, however, and some of the cases which follow rely almost exclusively on conversations with the person directly responsible for the program plus an evaluation of supporting documentation. The worksheet used in the field interviews is included in the Appendix.

The twelve case studies are presented in Chapters 2 through 13. Not all of these cases represent rigorous scientific experiments; the "purist" will find a number of grounds on which to be critical. Many of these experiments lack adequate control groups or rigorous statistical tests of changes. The criteria of productivity change vary from one case to the next. In almost all of the cases, the changes can be attributed to multiple causes, and it is impossible to single out precisely what the main effects are. In some of the studies, we found a certain amount of overstatement in the published literature and the actual results were more modest than depicted.

But, we have not dwelled upon these factors which might be criticized by a "purist"; at the same time, we have tried not to go beyond the scientific evidence and to report faithfully what was done and what the results were. In our view, these twelve cases present an impressive series of experiences in changing some aspect of the way in which the human resource is managed in these twelve organizations. All of the cases reflect positive, measurable, and significant effects upon some aspects of human resource productivity.

In most of the cases dealt with in this book, the actual organizations are identified, and the persons participating in the experiments are identified by their real names. In a few of the cases pseudonyms and fictitious company names are used. All of the quotations, however, are the actual comments of members of the organizations described.

The twelve case studies may be classified under three broad categories in terms of the types of innovations which were made. Four of the organizations undertook changes which can be classified in broad terms as "behavioral." This means that the underlying rationale for the changes can be found in behavioral psychology and that the changes consisted of efforts to reinforce positively valued behaviors through systematic management of rewards and reinforcements. These include experiments dealing with the process of setting performance goals, providing feedback about progress made toward goal attainment, and rewarding the types of behaviors which contribute to productivity.

Four of the other cases may be categorized broadly as belonging to what we have called a "humanistic" orientation. In these cases, the primary emphasis has been on creating an environment which encourages workers' active participation and commitment toward achieving the goals of the organization. This orientation is one which explicitly recognizes and attempts to draw out and sustain the workers' commitment to increasing productivity and high performance.

The final four cases in this book involve changes which primarily may be viewed as "structural." Here, basic conditions associated with the design of jobs and with the design of working conditions were changed in such a way that they led to greater employee motivation, commitment, or efficiency.

Allocating the twelve studies among these three categories was not all that precise a process. First of all, there is a certain amount of conceptual fuzziness and overlapping across the categories. The processes of goal setting and feedback, which we have tended to place in the area of "behavioral" experiments, often included participation by employees in the decision process. Structural changes in the design of work also often included participation. One of the common aspects of job design is to build in feedback from the work flow so that workers are able to evaluate their performance and adjust their goals if necessary. Thus, many of the experiments included elements which could be thought of as behavioral, humanistic, *and* structural.

However, there is a primary thrust to each of the cases, and we have allocated them to one of the three categories based upon this thrust. The "behaviorally oriented" case studies are contained in

Chapters 2 through 5. Chapters 6 through 9 cover the four "humanistically oriented" case studies. Finally, Chapters 10 through 13 cover the four cases in which "structural" changes were the predominant theme of the experiment.

Chapter 2 deals with a program installed in the bakery operations of a large supermarket distribution center in Detroit which had been experiencing severe absenteeism problems. The program entailed an incentive program using a variable reinforcement schedule built around a poker game for on-time attendance. For each on-time day, each worker received a card. After five consecutive days, the highest poker hands received an incentive payment. The results were clearly positive in increasing attendance in the bakery operations, and they were cost effective.

Chapter 3 deals with a program of regular management feedback to employees about production and quality in a small diecasting plant in the Midwest. The program was designed to systematically use positive reinforcement, encouragement, and goal setting, as well as feedback. This program resulted in significant savings to the company.

In Chapter 4, a program of goal setting and positive reinforcement in the Building Maintenance, Motor Vehicle Maintenance, and Supply function of Michigan Bell Telephone Company is described. From relatively low performance levels prior to implementation of the program, in over three years the unit of Michigan Bell in which the program was implemented has moved to a position at the top of the system and continues to improve.

Chapter 5 describes a comprehensive research program dealing with the goal-setting process and with different schedules of reinforcement in the Weyerhaeuser Company in Tacoma, Washington. Positive results with significant productivity increases have been obtained in lumbering operations in Oklahoma, in tree planting in North Carolina, and in Washington State among mountain beaver trappers. Other studies have been conducted among typists in word processing centers and among scientists and engineers in research and development laboratories.   The results of these studies are a dramatic demonstration of the productivity yields which can be obtained from implementation of basic behavioral approaches.

Chapter 6 represents the first of the "humanistic" experiments. It involves the installation of a participative system of management in a large aerospace company in California. Over a period of several years, a systematic attempt to increase employee participation in decision making and to open up channels of communication resulted in significant productivity enhancements through improved product quality and production in the manufacture of missile guidance systems.

In Chapter 7, the experiences in participatively designing an incentive plan for attendance at the Sanitary Group—a small building services and cleaning company in New Haven, Connecticut—are described. Poor attendance in the building services crews had been causing severe problems to the company in servicing its clients. The employees were asked to design an incentive plan and once the plan was implemented, attendance improved significantly. The results were not as dramatic in a comparison group in which an incentive plan was imposed without employee participation.

Chapter 8 describes a continuing effort at the XYZ plant of the AHM Corporation to build improved labor/management cooperation through joint problem solving and openness of communication. The approach is a "humanistic" one of trying to enhance understanding between labor and management and to gain more involvement, sharing of objectives, and commitment to improve the operation. The productivity results have been substantial, including dramatic reductions in grievances and absenteeism.

Chapter 9, the final of the "humanistic" case studies, describes how, over a period of two years, a new plant manager has changed the climate and functioning of a small paint manufacturing plant in East Moline, Illinois. The company is the Valspar Corporation. The new manager, who had had direct experience with the widely publicized innovative program of management at the Topeka, Kansas, plant of General Foods Corporation, worked directly to increase the trust level of employees, to open communications, to increase employee involvement in decision making, and in general to improve the quality of working life in the plant. Over the two years there have been significant improvements in product quality, decreases in employee turnover (from a high of 187 percent to a negligible amount), and decreased absenteeism.

Chapter 10 describes the process of implementing flexible working hours in the SmithKline Corporation in Philadelphia—a change which we have termed "structural." While actual productivity was not measured in this study, the perceptions of both supervisors and employees were that there were significant productivity gains from variable working hours. In addition, there were positive effects on absenteeism and a reduction in overtime. The attitudes of employees were highly favorable to the flexible working hours program.

Chapter 11 describes a structural change in a large technology project—the systems programming effort of IBM in Poughkeepsie, New York. At Poughkeepsie, the traditional form of organization was changed from that of individual programmers working on segments of a large computer program to a team structure. The teams also made possible better utilization of skills because appropriate support personnel were assigned to the teams along with the programmers. In addition, a peer review system was instituted to try to enhance the quality of the programming code being written in the large-scale programs. The results were highly positive, particularly in terms of product quality.

Chapter 12 describes a job design experiment in a government agency—the Social Security Administration in Baltimore, Maryland. Through structural changes in the nature of the work in several large clerical departments, it was possible to obtain significant productivity increases in an operation that seemingly had little potential for improvement.

Chapter 13 also deals with a series of job design experiments and programs at the Air Logistics Center at Hill Air Force Base in Ogden, Utah. Here, a program of "orthodox job enrichment" has been promoted extensively by Professor Frederick Herzberg of the University of Utah over the last several years. Over 3,000 employees have been involved in the program, covering approximately 100 positions. The carefully audited return in terms of savings and productivity amounts to over $2 million. The orthodox job enrichment program at the Ogden Air Logistics Center seems close to becoming a self-sustaining institutionalized program of organizational improvement in the human resource area to enhance productivity through structural changes in the nature of work.

The concluding chapter of the book—Chapter 14—draws out the

common threads from these twelve cases and attempts to outline the factors that have been responsible for the successes and the failures included among them. A strategy for enhancing productivity through better human resource utilization, as well as for enhancing the quality of working life, is outlined in this chapter.

2

A Poker Game Incentive
for Attendance*

One of the basic tenets of psychology is that rewarded behavior tends to repeat itself. This principle is at the core of the psychology of learning and development.

By using this principle, some action strategies for the organization having productivity problems may be tied to the behavior of its work force. First of all, the organization should make every effort to change problem behaviors into a more desirable and productive pattern. The key to this change is to focus directly on the behavior and its consequences and not on employee attitudes or opinions. Then, if desirable behavior is rewarded appropriately, there is a reasonable chance that the behavioral pattern will change and that the change will "stick."

The case that follows is the story of such an attempt to change an undesirable behavioral pattern into a more productive pattern. The unproductive behavior was absenteeism, and the organization initiating the experiment was a food distribution and manufacturing company in the Midwest. The approach to the problem was both very novel and very successful.

There is also an interesting corollary story to this case. First of all, the primary motivation to initiate the program—at least on the part of the individual who designed and conducted it—was not to solve a pressing organizational problem. Rather, the motive of the person responsible for the program was to demonstrate the potential for changing behavior in an organizational setting through the application of appropriate psychological principles. His hope, then, was to

*Pedalino, E. and Gamboa, V. U., Behavior modification and absenteeism: Intervention in one industrial setting. *J. Appl. Psychol.* 59 (6): 694–698 (Dec. 1974).

use this demonstration to gain entrée for other work in various parts of the organization.

Secondly, the unit of this organization which was willing—in fact eager—to undertake the program was precisely the unit with the least problem of productivity and absenteeism. This unit was not absolutely problem free, but, in a relative sense at least, they were well off.

There is an unwritten "law" of human resource management: Organizations with the fewest problems are the most receptive to stepping up to them and dealing with them creatively. Conversely, organizations in deep trouble most typically are nonreceptive to basic changes in their human resource management system. The case we are about to describe is an active demonstration of this tendency.

In May 1972, Ed Pedalino became training manager at the manufacturing and distribution center of a large food marketing organization in the Midwest. There were roughly 1,800 employees in the center. The plant was located in a large predominantly blue collar urban community and was the second largest employer in the community.

The distribution center consisted of ten plants which, for all practical purposes, were independent of one another. These plants covered such activities as manufacturing, dairy, bakery, warehouse, produce, and so forth—the various activities associated with food manufacturing and distribution centers.

Shortly after he assumed his position as training manager, Ed Pedalino searched for a setting in which to apply his skills as a resource person in enhancing the utilization of human resources. His intention was to find a manager of one of the plants who would be receptive to trying some of the concepts from behavioral psychology which he brought with him to his new job. It was a typical process of a new professional employee trying to build a role for himself in an ongoing organization.

As Ed recalls it, "Before long, I had a nibble from the manager in the bakery department. He was concerned about problems of absenteeism and asked to confer with me about what might be done about the situation."

Ed began to work with this manager and undertook a detailed analysis of absenteeism data. "As it turned out, however, this manager had the lowest absence by far of any of the plants. But he still wanted to do something about it, so I agreed to work with him."

As Ed investigated the absenteeism problem, it became clear that even though the overall rate of absenteeism was not excessive in comparison with some of the other plants, it was injecting some serious problems in the operations of the bakery. "The fact is, you just didn't know when they would take off. They had a three-day weekend every so often. The problem is, you never knew when "every so often" would be."

Part of the problem, Ed concluded, revolved around the sick day policy included in the union contract. While it was possible for individuals to "bank" up to six days of sick time each year, up to a total of fifty-five days to be used in the event of serious illness, there was no motivation in the work force to do this. The average age of the bakery employees was only twenty-nine years, and they were not interested in the security of a "bank" of potential sick days; instead, they took the days whenever it was convenient.

Ed also determined that supervisors placed little emphasis on attendance in their single-minded attention to day-to-day production concerns. As a result, the frequency of explanatory notes from employees who were absent and supervisory checking on the reasons was "less than 100 percent." He decided that a program of clarification and feedback might be helpful in reducing the absenteeism rate. To achieve this, he designed a novel type of incentive program.

Ed is quick to point out that while this type of program was perfectly appropriate for the population of employees he was dealing with, it might not be appropriate in all settings. Specifically, this incentive and feedback system revolved around a poker game. As there was high interest in lotteries and card games among the employees in the distribution center, the plan which Ed devised generated considerable interest and involvement in this particular work group. It might very well fall flat with a different, less interested employee population.

The program was designed so that an employee was allowed to choose a card from a deck of playing cards on each day that he came to work on time. At the end of the five-day week each employee had five cards—a normal poker hand. The highest hand won twenty dollars. There were eight winners each week, one winner from approximately each department in the plant. The rules of the game were straightforward:

1) You must be a full time hourly employee in the bakery. 2) You must punch in on time (tardiness disqualifies you). 3) Lateness or sickness or any other reason for not being at work makes you ineligible to play. 4) You must have five cards to win (five working days on time). 5) If the above conditions are met you will be able to choose a card from a poker deck—during your shift, from your supervisor. 6) The card you have chosen will be recorded by your supervisor on a score sheet and score chart. 7) The winners will receive money on Sunday after work. 8) The same card may be used more than once.

The rules for winning—the standard poker rules, adding the possibility for five cards of the same kind—were also clarified. The regular days off for the bakery were Tuesday and Saturday (except for maintenance crews); payoff from the poker incentive was scheduled for Sunday after work.

A large chart was placed within each department in the bakery on which each employee's poker hand was posted as it evolved each week. Each day of absence was marked on the chart with a large red "A," and an "L" for late was written on any days the employee was late. Thus, there was very clear feedback to all employees, both about how the open hand of poker was progressing as well as their record with regard to attendance and tardiness. The involvement of the employees in the game was very evident, and there was some side betting as the cards were drawn.

For a thirty-two week period before the lottery was launched, the overall weekly absenteeism rate averaged 3.01 percent. The target for the lottery program was to reduce that rate to 2.31 percent. This was determined by computing what the absenteeism rate would be if all employees took just their six sick days of leave each year. The target was seen as feasible as the absenteeism rate in some weeks had been below that level even without the incentive program.

During the sixteen weeks that the experiment was in effect, absenteeism dropped to an average of 2.46 percent. This represented an 18.3 percent decline in absenteeism from the base rate: a significant decline. While the goal line of 2.31 was not achieved, the experiment did produce significant savings and a reduction of absenteeism.

For the first six weeks of the experiment the poker game lottery was held every week. Then, the intention was to stretch out the schedule so that the game was held only every other week, and this schedule was to be maintained for the last ten weeks.

Inadvertently, however, the lottery was omitted in one of the weeks in which it should have been held during the second part of the experiment. As a result, there were three straight weeks during which no lottery was held. When this happened, absenteeism immediately increased from 2.3 percent to 3.9 percent. Presumably, the interval for maintaining the incentive for good attendance had been stretched beyond the point where it was effective. Significantly, however, when the incentive was again put into place absenteeism immediately dropped to 2.4 percent and stayed at that relatively low level for the next six weeks until the end of the experiment. This accidental omission of one of the scheduled poker games helps to illustrate the effectiveness of the incentive for decreasing absenteeism.

The results also suggested that the incentive effect was real, not a "Hawthorne" effect or a passing interest. There was a tendency for absences to begin to build up on Thursday, Friday, and Sunday. Presumably, as the poker hand began to evolve, some people saw that they had little chance of winning and thus the incentive for attendance was less strong later in the week than it was earlier in the week. (Perhaps using a high/low poker hand might have overcome this tendency.)

It was also evident that the plan did not always work. For example, on the Tuesday after Labor Day, absences were significantly higher than they were during the other weeks of the experiment; the money incentives involved were just not enough to overcome the desire for stretching out the Labor Day holiday a little longer. These trends emphasize the fact that it is important not only to know what is rewarding to individuals but also the relative value of the rewards when designing a behavioral change strategy.

Even though the program seemed to be very successful in reducing absenteeism, and it was considered to be cost effective in terms of the cost of the incentive versus the savings from better attendance, it was discontinued after the sixteen-week trial period. There probably were several reasons for the discontinuance of the program. For one, Ed Pedalino recalls, one of the union stewards brought up the question of gambling on the premises and expressed some concern about that aspect of the program. Also, some of the supervisor's thoughts on the program were summed up in the comments by one supervisor who stated: "Hey, I have to hand twenty dollars to that damn guy for coming to work. It doesn't seem right." Some of the other supervisors, however, thought the program was "a great idea," or that it "put a little life into this place," and so forth.

But the major reason the program was stopped after sixteen weeks was because contract negotiations were coming up and management did not want the incentive program to be written into the union contract. Therefore, the experiment was abandoned after the sixteen-week trial period.

Attendance was tracked during a twenty-two week follow-up period after the system was phased out. Absenteeism during that period climbed to 3.02 percent; an increase of 30.1 percent over the rate during the trial period. It was very clear that the program was responsible for reducing absenteeism, and when it was removed, absenteeism returned to its former level.

During the period of the trial, it is significant that absenteeism in four comparison departments actually increased 13.8 percent; in the bakery, on the other hand, during the trial period absenteeism was reduced by 18.3 percent. Clearly the incentive was instrumental in reducing absenteeism, at least during the short run sixteen-week period.

This case illustrates the application of behavioral analysis and design in attempting to shape behavior on the job—in this case attendance. The approach recognizes that all job activities have associated with them various sets of consequences to the individual. For most activities, there is a mixture of both positive and negative probable outcomes. In the case of attendance, for example, positive outcomes might include an opportunity to work on a challenging assignment, contact with enjoyable peers, or supervisory approval. The positive outcomes from attendance must be balanced against perceived positive outcomes from absenteeism: time for golf, less fatigue, etc. There is a similar balance of negative consequences associated both with attendance and with absenteeism.

The analysis of behavioral consequences attempts to identify as many of these potential outcomes as possible. Then, systems are designed to introduce as many positive consequences into the desired job activity as possible.

In this case study it was determined that the excitement of a lottery or poker game would be positively valued by most members of the work force. The potential money award was also positively valued, though the lottery aspect increased its probable value.

Other strategies might have been tried as well: making the work more challenging, providing better working facilities, supervisory recognition, incentives, etc. But, the analysis of behavioral consequences suggested that this particular design would be especially appropriate in this specific organizational setting. And it worked!

Other case examples, in which the behavioral consequences associated with various job activities were systematically altered to enhance performance, are included in some of the later chapters. But for now the preceding example of handling an absenteeism problem in the supermarket distribution center provides us with some good illustrative guidelines for taking a behaviorally oriented approach to enhancing productivity. The various steps which an organization should go through and the types of questions which should be asked include the following.

1. Is there a problem of productivity in the organization which can be traced to specific patterns of employee behavior? This may include such things as indifference to quality, excessive scrap, turnover, unsafe practices, grievances, as well as low levels of production.
2. Then, an analysis of the consequences of these behaviors needs to be made. Why is it that employees behave in this fashion? What are the positive returns which accrue to them which override any benefits of alternate patterns of behavior? In the case of the supermarket distribution center, employees very often perceived more personal return from staying away from work than from coming to work. The question to be asked in a systematic fashion is "Why?"
3. Next, the analysis should try to identify whether or not the consequences of behavior can be changed to tip the balance in

favor of an alternate desired pattern of behavior. Ed Pedalino felt that the possibility of a twenty dollar poker game incentive, and the fun of participating in the game, might be sufficient in many cases to offset the desire for personal time and leisure. In large measure, he was right.

4. In searching for alternatives which can change the consequences of behavior, the behavioral analyst must be sure that the elements he comes up with fit in with the values and culture of the employee group with which he is dealing. The analyst also has to be sure that the changes are large enough to be perceived as meaningful. Installing a poker game incentive for attendance seemed clearly appropriate with the workers at the supermarket distribution center in Detroit; if the same incentive were used in the Bible Belt of the rural South it might even have a negative effect—as one of our subsequent cases demonstrates. The behavioral analyst must search for altered consequences—rewards or reinforcements—which are meaningful to the group of employees under consideration.

5. An analysis of cost effectiveness is needed. Obviously, behavioral consequences can be altered to the point where they will change almost any pattern of behavior if enough money is spent—few people would refuse to come to work for a $1,000 per day incentive. Therefore, the point of return on investment from an alternate set of consequences needs to be determined. At the same time, the incentive has to be large enough to be meaningful to the individuals concerned. It should be recognized, however, as some of our later cases illustrate, that there is not always a direct monetary cost involved in changing behavioral consequences. Nonmonetary incentives such as feedback, recognition, praise, or sense of accomplishment can often be built into the job situation and serve as incentives to behavior change. Part of this concern with cost effectiveness must look at potential negative consequences to the organization from the change. In the bakery illustration management was unwilling to continue with the program, even though it was cost effective, because they did not want it written into the union contract. These kinds of contingencies should be explored and dealt with in any type of behavioral analysis and program design.

6. Finally, a program to change the consequences of behavior and thus enhance productivity should be tested to be sure that the analysis and design behind the changes are sound and, in fact, that they work. Then, after a successful test, the changes can be implemented more broadly.

Behavioral technology such as that illustrated by the bakery case can be extremely powerful if applied in a systematic well-analyzed fashion. Most organizations have barely scratched the surface of the potential productivity improvements that could be made from carefully analyzing the behavioral consequences of organizational problems and attempting to restructure or counterbalance those consequences with other outcomes which tend to shape behavior in a direction desired for organizational effectiveness.

3
Enhancing Product Quality*

Social commentators who take the "big picture" view of the twen-
tieth century industrial scene versus the world of work a hundred or
more years ago very quickly arrive at several basic conclusions. First
of all—and certainly there is no refuting this—the productivity of the
average American worker has risen dramatically. New production
technologies, better management, and economies of scale, all so
much a part of the industrial scene over the last hundred years, and
particularly over the last fifty years, all contribute to make American
enterprise today the most productive in history.

At the same time, many social commentators would come to the
opposite conclusion with regard to work quality. Although the facts
of the matter are somewhat less obvious than with regard to productivity, there is a rather pervasive feeling that many of our modern
production technologies have eroded craftsmanship and have tended
to foster a degree of shoddy workmanship which would not have
been acceptable in former years. There is certainly some face validity
for this position; witness the planned obsolescence of many of our
products, the growing need for a consumer protectionist movement,
and a very evident "I don't care" attitude among many workers.

Problems of poor quality may arise from volume production,
fractionated work assignments, and general feelings of lack of commitment and alienation on the part of the workers. While poor
quality can result from defective parts or from defective tooling,
most often the root causes of quality problems lie in human resource
factors. Although production is relatively easy to control—through

*Adam, E. E., Jr., Behavior modification in quality control. *Acad. Manag. J.* 18(4): 662–
679 (Dec. 1975).

the pace of an assembly line or through production targets which are readily counted—controlling or improving quality very often depends upon motivational factors: making people care.   Improving the quality also often requires making sure that workers are aware of the quality of the goods they are producing.

Although there is an old industrial engineering precept of separating quality control from production, more and more it is becoming recognized that motivationally this does nothing to support good quality. If workers are unaware of the quality of the product they are turning out, how can they then correct problems and improve?

Quality is an important part of productivity. Scrap is costly. And finally, customer dissatisfaction with poor quality goods can, in the final analysis, make or break an organization. The extent to which an organization can increase the quality of its products will have a direct impact on productivity and profitability.

In recent years we have seen growing interest in increasing product quality. For example, zero defects programs have been adopted in many organizations to directly improve the quality and reliability of their products. These programs originated in the aerospace industry where high reliability was essential, but similar approaches have been adopted by other organizations. Zero defects programs tend to be efforts to change the attitudes of the workforce so that workers are directly motivated to produce goods of high quality.

Similarly, many job enrichment experiments have dealt with, among other things, the quality control aspects of the production process. One of the factors often associated with successful job enrichment experiments is to give production operators responsibility for quality inspection and control as well as for production.

A small diecasting company in the Midwest recently took a somewhat different approach in attempting to increase quality in its operations. The company felt that the number of poor quality diecasting shots was above what was desirable, resulting in inadequate machine usage and excessive scrap and remelt. The company was also concerned about the amount of rework required from poor quality materials being passed on to subsequent machining operations from the diecasting department.

The diecasting industry is highly competitive. Because of the considerable expense of diecasting equipment and the cost of rework, anything which increases the yield of good castings can make a substantial contribution to productivity and to profitability.

Diecasting is an operation in which the operator can be expected to have some control over yields. There are several operations involved in a diecasting shot. First, the operator cleans and lubricates the die. Then the die is closed, and the operator ladles molten aluminum or zinc and pours it into the die. He then triggers the plunger to force the metal into the die and after an appropriate interval releases the completed casting and repeats the cycle.

The breakoff man—the operator who breaks off excess metal from the casting—immediately sees whether or not the cast is of good quality. He is in the position to provide feedback about quality directly to the operator. However, some quality problems such as porosity or hidden voids are not discovered by the breakoff man but show up in later processing and in machining.

Tom Richey, who was quality control manager at the midwestern diecasting company, points out how quality can be effected by the way in which the operator carries out the sequence of operations involved in making a diecasting shot.

> The easiest thing to improve on the diecasting machine is speed, as opposed to quality. A lot of times you get the benefit of quality, though. The faster the machine runs, the hotter the die. And the hotter the die, the better the casting. But even more importantly, the more consistently you run the machine, the better casting you'll get. You have to be up to a good hot die before you're going to get a good casting.

Experienced operators develop a natural rhythm for their work. They know when the machine is running at an optimal speed and temperature and time the various components of the diecasting shot based upon their experience with this rhythm.

In early 1974 the company had forty-three operators assigned to three different shifts operating manually controlled diecasting machines. A number of these people were relatively inexperienced, and their yields of good castings were lower than the yields of experienced operators. As a result, the company was receptive to an experimental proposal developed by a professor from a nearby university whose purpose was to undertake field experimentation on various ways of increasing productivity.

Starting from some work done in research laboratories, the professor proposed to the company that they initiate a program to improve quality which would test the effectiveness of two different approaches. First of all, there was to be an effort to change workers' attitudes about quality through various procedures similar to those used in zero defects programs. Secondly, he proposed testing what he termed "operant conditioning" procedures. These procedures were to be a direct effort on the part of supervision in the plant to provide regular feedback to the workers about levels of quality, to reward workers through praise and encouragement for good levels of quality, and gradually to "shape" workers' behavior toward consistent good quality performance through systematic feedback and rewards. The researcher's primary purpose was to compare these two approaches toward quality improvement; the organization's purpose was to help the researcher and also to improve quality and production if possible.

To initiate the program, the researcher was introduced to the employees at a meeting and the purpose of the program was explained. The union was thoroughly briefed and understood the purpose. Then, the researcher talked with each of the three shift foremen individually and explained in detail what was to be done.

Basically, he asked them to talk with each operator each week and review the results from the previous week in some detail. He provided a suggestion of the way in which the conversation should be approached but told them to structure their own feedback sessions in detail in the way that was most comfortable to them personally. The discussion, which was designed to emphasize quality results and also talk about quantity, was outlined as follows:

FOREMAN/OPERATOR DISCUSSION

The following is intended to be a general guide for foremen to follow when discussing quality with the operator. It has three parts:

1. Quantity and quality results
2. Quality emphasis
3. Informal discussion

1) *Quantity and Quality Results.*   As foreman you want to convey information to your subordinate concerning his quantity and quality of work and how he compares to the average. You will give him weekly summaries of *his average*, *the shift average*, and *the department average* for *percent performance* and *pieces scrap*. I might say something like this:

> Tom, we are taking a few minutes to go over weekly production figures. I would like to share them with you. First let me show you your percent performance, which is your percent of standards shots. It was _____ percent last week. Your number of scrap pieces was _____ .
>
> I've got these same figures for our shift average and the department average. The shift averaged _____ percent performance and _____ scrap pieces per man. The department averaged _____ percent performance and _____ scrap pieces per man.

2) *Quality Emphasis.*   The purpose of this part of your discussion is to focus on the man's overall quality. The main information you have are the scrap pieces given above for *him*, *the shift*, and *the department*. I might say something like this:

> Tom, let's look at your scrap pieces again. You had _____ scrap pieces. This was (*above, about, below*) the shift average. Your scrap pieces performance is (*poor, satisfactory, very good*).

Then if performance was poor (high scrap):

> Tom, we can improve your scrap pieces. I'd like to see you try to do better next week and I'll give you the figures then again.

Then if performance was satisfactory (average scrap):

> Tom, you are doing a good job. I'd like to see you be below the average shift scrap pieces. I think you can do it. I'll give you the figures again next week.

Then if performance was very good (below average scrap):

> Tom, you are doing a fine job on your scrap. I'd like to see you stay below the shift average. I'll give you your scrap figures again next week.

As the program develops you will want to change the quality emphasis somewhat. An *average* for a shift or department means some will usually be below or above that average. If the department or shift average scrap pieces starts declining, it is not fair to go back to a low performer—who is improving and lowering the scrap average—and again and again stress he is "below average." Shift your emphasis a little, giving him some praise for improvement—but *only if he has improved*.

Remember, the focus is on quality. If percent performance starts to drop, discuss that but we are *emphasizing scrap pieces*.

3) *Informal Discussion.*   Ask for questions. Here is where you will learn what the operator *perceives* his quality problems are. Remember, your perception and his perception might not be the same. Sometimes both are different than the real cause for scrap. Together, you talk over his scrap performance in the manner and style that is most comfortable for you. Try to leave the discussion on a *positive* note. The purpose is to encourage better performance through verbally relating his actual performance with average or standard performance. Praise or negative comments are a part of this, but try to end the discussion positively. I might end it with:

> Tom, I've gotten something from our talk and I'm looking forward to next week's performance figures.

Gene Harvey, the first shift foreman at the plant, recalls that he would usually talk with his operators on Tuesday or Wednesday rather than on a Monday which was most often a "hectic day." He would take them to a metallurgical office out on the shop floor and sit down for ten minutes or so and go through the results for the previous week. The computer report on weekly results dealing with the number of hours that each machine ran, the number of diecasting shots, scrap, and the percentage yields would be the basis for that discussion. Gene would be positive in his approach saying, "You did a good job" and offer encouragement. He stated that he followed the outline presented by the researcher relatively closely and felt that the foremen on the other shifts did as well.

Harvey recalls that he would often discuss problems the operators were having with specific dies, and sometimes he would then be in a position to help them out with their problems by sending the die back to tooling for rework. He explained how the process would operate.

> Say a person is getting 60 percent. He knows that you know it's a problem with the die, and if you ask him to try to do better, he'll try. And if it's only 1 or 2 percent more, the ten minute conversation would be well worth it. Even if it didn't help, at least he knew that you were aware of the problem and that he wasn't laying down on the job. It makes a person feel good to try to do a better job.

Production quotas for most of the diecasting runs were set against standards for each job. Standards specified the number of diecasting shots which were to be made per hour. Harvey recalls:

> Sometimes a person would say the job was rated too high. I'd have a feel for that, though, and I'd say, "I know, Joe, it's rated way too high at 120, but I think you should get 100 pieces an hour. If you get 100 pieces an hour, I'll back you up if anybody says anything," which I did. He'd say, "Hell, I can't make it, it's crazy." And I'd tell him, "Well, Joe, I think I could run it at that speed, and I think you could because I know you're as good an operator as I am, and probably better." Whether they were or not, that's beside the point. He'd come up with more shots. Now certain people—hell you couldn't motivate them with dynamite. Most people will come through for you when you put it to them that way, though.

> The sessions were supposed to take ten minutes. Sometimes they'd run into twenty or twenty-five minutes. You'd get them talking, and sometimes you'd run into their own personal problems.

So, in effect, the "operant conditioning" program designed to focus on quality became a process of regular conversation between the foreman and the worker each week about performance and a range of other topics.

Tom Richey recalls:

> Nobody had ever sat down with these foremen and told them you should do this or anything. They were told to communicate with

their people. That to me was one of the immediate advantages of the program. Sit down with the people to help them. I don't think it would make any difference if you sat down to talk with them about their children instead of performance, but it just got them interested.

During the course of the program, a series of other activities designed to encourage workers to focus directly on quality were instituted. A banner was displayed in the diecasting department with the slogan: "Quality Counts." In addition, a large graph was installed showing the percent production and scrap pieces for the overall department by the week. An insert emphasizing quality was included with the paycheck. Also, a wall graph was eventually installed showing production and scrap pieces for each shift by week.

In Gene Harvey's view, however, "there wasn't much said about the slogans and charts and so forth. Quantity was emphasized about as much as quality."

The program ran for thirty-six weeks. At that point it was decided to implement the program plantwide, and an intended comparison of the diecasting department versus the machining department, which was designated to serve as a "control group" in which no changes were made, was no longer possible. Therefore, to evaluate the results, quantity and quality data for a period of seven weeks before the program started were compared with similar data during the last seven weeks of the program.

There were forty-three operators on three diecasting shifts at the start of the program and forty-one at the conclusion. Between these two periods, which spanned forty-three weeks, the percent of scrap in the diecasting departments increased very slightly from 5.53 in the first seven weeks to 5.99 in the last seven weeks. While this was not a significant increase, it certainly did not reflect the kind of improvement that had been hoped for as a result of the emphasis on quality.

However, *quantity* increased significantly over the same period. The quantity was expressed in terms of percentage performance against the production standard. This measure increased from 90.91 percent to 96.58 percent, a statistically significant increase. Production went up on all three of the diecasting shifts.

The company figures that the net value from changes in quantity and quality as a result of the program amounted to $1,543 per week.

This totals $77,177 annually. So, clearly, the program produced real and tangible productivity benefits for the company.

In the face of these demonstrated results, then, it is interesting that in late 1976 the program was no longer in operation in this die-casting company. Why?

Gene Harvey provides some insights:

We did it all through 1975 until July 1976. Then, after vacation, things got hairy, and it slipped. We haven't been doing it lately, but the only reason we haven't—well, we don't have that many people, right now. We've only got two operators per shift, and the operators we've got usually come up with 100 percent regardless. They're guys that have worked here for twenty or twenty-five years. A lot of the other people had only been here six months to a year or two years, and you really don't learn it all—not in that period of time. But with only two operators, we can talk with them informally.

Since 1974, most of the diecasting operation in the company has been automated. New equipment has replaced the need for operator control on the manual machines and at the same time has reduced the need for the kind of feedback program which had been demonstrated to be so effective. With the automated machines, the process is run at a fast rate, the dies are kept hot, and the quality yields tend to be universally high.

George Wisninski, Vice-President of operations in the company feels that:

We are missing a lot of the benefits in other departments where that kind of an approach could and should be applied. I think it's very worthwhile, but we can't impose it on the middle levels of management. If the others would have the same attitude as the bench foreman, I'd be all for it if they initiated that kind of feedback. But it has to initiate with the foreman.

He outlines how in one of the departments, final processing and bench inspection, the forewoman has adopted the practice of talking regularly with the workers. As a result of these talks production has increased and results are excellent. It is not an official program and there is no publicity to it, but this forewoman has used it to build excellent rapport with the employees and has achieved very high standards. Wisninski concludes that although there has been some spin-off from the original project, it could be greater.

Gene Harvey summarizes his feelings about the program:

It didn't make any spectacular difference, but it did help. Personally, I think it helped the people, because they figured we were at least interested in what was going on. It reduces tension in people when they get a chance to unload.

George Wisninski outlines a number of reasons why the program gradually faded. Most of these reasons revolve around change.

1. There is a new general foreman in the plant who was not involved in the original plan and is not particularly committed to the program.
2. The second shift foreman left, and his replacement was not involved and therefore not committed to the program. There has been no emphasis on the program on his part.
3. The quality control manager and quality assurance foreman have changed. The quality assurance foreman was supposed to be responsible for the program, but the new man did not pick it up when he moved into the job.
4. The program is not receiving any push from senior management.

Probably the major reason, however, is that the technology has changed. Only a few manual diecasting machines are still in use. In 1976 there were only nine operators versus more than forty at the time the project was tested. These nine operators are highly experienced people who obtain very good production results without a formal feedback program.

George Wisninski points out that the role of the researcher as a catalyst and mover to make the program work was also very important; he is no longer on the site.

There are several points which can be learned from this case study. First of all, it was a typical example of a field experiment. While the researcher primarily wanted to emphasize quality and study ways to improve quality, in the field situation one does not always have control over what is done. It is very clear that many of the discussions which the foremen had with the operators dealt very directly with quantity, as well as with quality. It is also clear that in this particular situation the two are inextricably bound together. The main thing that the operators could impact on these jobs was quantity of production. Presumably, at the same time quality yields were upheld, but much of the emphasis inevitably was on production.

It is also clear that in this program some of the positive benefits resulted from the good human relations created by just talking with people. The degree of direct foreman interest and support, on a regular basis, was new in the organization and undoubtedly served to enhance the motivation of the operators to perform well.

Gene Harvey sums up his feelings in this regard:

> I think probably a lot of the problems of industry today are that we don't operate close enough to the people. Not just the foremen, but the people who are higher than foreman. After a while I think the higher echelon feel you're just there to produce a part and if you don't produce a part then they'll get rid of you. Managers take employees for granted. Just like another machine. If you can't do a job, we'll get somebody else. And that won't solve the problem. It'll work less and less, because you can tell the difference with the younger people we're getting in today. They're not as tolerant as people of my age. They want to be recognized. True, you've got to produce a product, but you can't produce a product without people. If you produce good people, then you can produce good products.

The degree of change in this organization is also a factor in this case, particularly the degree of technology change as the diecasting process was automated and the need for operators reduced. The program which fit a particular situation and solved a problem became less and less appropriate as fewer operators were involved and as the level of experience and capability of the operators increased. Due to changes in technology, a program which worked very well under some circumstances no longer fit the circumstances. But, undoubtedly there are other circumstances in which such a program would "fit" very well.

The components of this case provide insights into areas where many organizations can enhance productivity through a simple process of feedback to employees who do not get regular systematic information about how effective they are in their work. Most organizations rely upon the performance appraisal process to achieve this. But this is not the kind of feedback which truly builds motivation; if anything, performance appraisal feedback is usually very general and most often so far removed from behaviors being evaluated that it has little motivational impact.

However, in many work situations it is possible to identify ways of giving feedback to employees on a more regular and timely basis. In the diecasting company, this involved changing the behavior of the foremen and refocusing their efforts so that they would work with their people to enhance performance. As the case points out, many times foremen are not aware that this is part of their job responsibility, and they are not aware of the potential benefits to be gained from systematically working with employees to shape their behavior toward enhancing job productivity. The diecasting company found a way to do this.

First of all, the foremen had the basic information available to them which they needed. There were weekly computer runs of performance for each shift and for each individual diecasting machine operator. Similar production data are available in many job situations in most organizations. The potential value of systematically feeding this information back, in a positive fashion, to employees should be recognized. Feedback can either be from the foreman, as in the diecasting company, or through the straightforward posting of production records. The important point is that one of the prerequisites needed for employees to improve their performance is some systematic and timely information about how they are doing so that a direction for change is provided.

Implicit in this, of course, is that the knowledge of results will lead to the setting of goals for improvement. One of our later cases deals with this issue and the theoretical implications of goal setting. This was clearly part of the process of feedback at the diecasting company.

The feedback about performance should be given in a positive fashion, as it was in the diecasting company. Criticism or blame for goals not met or substandard performance will predictably lead to defensiveness and discouragement on the part of the employees. Behavior is shaped toward desired objectives from positive reinforcement—praise, encouragement, and rewards.

Also, implicit in this case study is the process of opening communications and showing respect for and concern about the employee as an individual. As pointed out by Gene Harvey, this open communication was clearly a major component responsible, in large part, for the positive improvement in performance. While this aspect of the change in the diecasting company seems more in line with the types of activities we shall be discussing in later chapters under the general heading of "Humanistic Factors," it is perfectly appropriate and correct to include it here, as we have done, along with more behaviorally oriented approaches such as goal setting, feedback, and reinforcement. It is evident that the program of systematic feedback, positive reinforcement, and openness of communication at the diecasting company clearly had an impact on the productivity of employees and the subsequent cost effectiveness of the diecasting operation.

4
Positive Reinforcement to Enhance Performance*

One of the areas which has received an increasing amount of attention from applied behavioral science in recent years is the process of goal setting. In part this results from the recent attention management has paid to concepts such as business planning and management by objectives. But also, it springs from a considerable amount of research in psychological laboratories which has probed the relationships between factors associated with setting goals and performance on a variety of tasks.

For example, some research has evaluated the effects on performance of participation in setting performance goals versus having goals or objectives imposed. Other studies have assessed the implications of specific difficult but attainable goals, as opposed to setting goals of "do your best." And, finally, there have been studies of the implications of knowledge of results in attaining goals (or feedback) on performance.

The general conclusions from these laboratory studies are: that difficult but attainable goals are more effective than simple goals of "do your best"; that participation in setting goals does not improve performance over that registered with imposed goals; and that the knowledge of results or feedback is effective only to the extent that it can be used by the individual to evaluate progress in relation to goals already set, or to set new goals. In other words, the laboratory studies suggest that for performance feedback to be effective, it must function to help the individual to understand his or her progress in moving toward clearly defined goals.

*Kim, J. S. and Hamner, W. C., Effect of performance feedback and goal-setting on productivity and satisfaction in an organizational setting. *J. Appl. Psychol.* **61**: 48–57 (1976).

This latter conclusion is one of the more controversial conclusions from these laboratory studies of goal setting. Over a number of years, there has been considerable research in psychology demonstrating the positive effects of knowledge of results or feedback on performance. Consequently, it has become well accepted that feedback is the mechanism by which workers learn how to adjust their performance to match desired standards. Feedback is also considered to be an incentive in and of itself which generates increased effort. So, to conclude from the laboratory research that goal setting is a more important factor of performance than knowledge of results seemingly contradicts a considerable amount of other research. However, the laboratory research on goal setting does not discount the value of feedback in enhancing performance; it merely concludes that goals are the framework through which the feedback is evaluated and channeled.

Partially to clarify the controversy, and perhaps more to test the laboratory findings in a real-life setting, there has been growing attention to extending the studies of the goal-setting process into field settings. For example, in 1974, Michigan Bell Telephone Company undertook a study designed to sort out the differential effects of goal setting and feedback on work performance. In addition, the study evaluated the effectiveness of three different types of feedback: intrinsic feedback, extrinsic feedback, and combinations of the two types.

The study was done in one of the Buildings, Supplies, and Motor Equipment Divisions of Michigan Bell. At the time of the study there were approximately 220 workers employed in 6 districts; 60 percent of these were blue-collar unionized employees and 40 percent were women. They were assigned to 3 different departments within each of the districts. Building maintenance personnel, including technicians and cleaners, maintained 72 buildings totaling over 2 million square feet which housed over 8000 Bell employees. A group of automobile mechanics maintained a fleet of over 1400 vehicles. And, finally, a third department administered an inventory of parts and supplies, backing up telephone installers.

In late 1973 the Metropolitan North area, which is the part of Michigan Bell in which the study was conducted, had not met any of four performance measures which were routinely evaluated. These performance measures were: safety, attendance, service, and costs.

The cost, attendance, and safety measures were based upon objective and quantitative information and expressed as a percentage of standard. The measure of service was developed from subjective ratings by the foremen.

In late 1973 Don Burwell was assigned as a new manager of the Metropolitan North Buildings, Supplies, and Motor Equipment Division. At that time he was also enrolled in an MBA program at Michigan State University. Don saw his new job assignment as an opportunity to test some of the concepts which were being covered in his master's degree program, and he used this as a thesis project for his degree. Of course, Don was also highly motivated to improve the performance of his new division and insure that performance measures were met in the future. So, working with some of the faculty members from the university, he designed a study to test systematic goal setting and positive reinforcement during a ninety-day trial.

Four different groups were identified for the study. Group #1 consisted of thirty-seven employees in two districts of the division engaged in building and motor vehicle maintenance. These employees, who were assigned to six work groups, were designated as an "extrinsic only" group. That is, employees in this group were to receive feedback about their performance from their supervisor on a regular basis. Each Monday morning, the six foremen were to meet with their groups and inform them of how many of the workers in the group had met the weekly goals during the previous week. At the same meeting, goals were to be set and emphasized for the current week. Also, at some time during the week the foreman was to visit each employee in his group and provide praise regarding those performance categories which exceeded the performance of the previous week. These were to be informal feedback sessions of short duration. The foremen specifically were not allowed to give negative feedback during this session.

Thus, the emphasis was to be on:

1. setting specific goals for each week;
2. providing group feedback about how the group had performed as compared to the goals set the previous week;
3. providing individualized positive reinforcement and feedback on an informal basis to each employee.

The second group was termed "intrinsic only" and consisted of building and motor vehicle maintenance employees assigned to two other districts. These twenty-six employees were assigned to six work groups. Each Monday morning, the six foremen were to meet with their groups to set goals for the week or to reemphasize the goals which had been set previously. There was not to be any feedback from the foreman about previous performance. However, on Friday of each week the workers were to rate themselves in terms of their own performance with regard to the various areas of measurement:

- Absenteeism
- Safety
- Cost control
- Quality of service

They used the same forms for these ratings as the foreman used and were given considerable instruction on how to compute the indices. The employees were told to keep the forms for their own use. Thus, this was a form of self-generated feedback which resulted in the knowledge of results and therefore, termed "intrinsic."

A third group was set up of twenty-six employees belonging to six different work groups. These employees were concerned with the supply function and operated in all six of the districts. Workers in these groups received both intrinsic and extrinsic feedback. Each Monday, the foremen met with the people they supervised and established goals or reemphasized already established goals for the week. On Friday, the employees filled out their own rating forms, and the foremen used these forms on the next Monday as a basis for the group feedback and goal-setting session. Also, during the week the foremen praised each worker individually on areas of performance which were successful and where goals had been met. Again, only positive reinforcement was permitted in these informal individualized sessions.

The fourth group was to serve as a control. This group consisted of twenty-four employees in two other districts involved with the building and automotive maintenance functions. On each Monday morning the foremen of this group were to meet with the workers they supervised to reemphasize weekly performance goals which had not changed and to explain any new goals. There was to be no specific feedback to the groups, either formally or informally.

Before instituting the program there was extensive training for the foremen in how to feed back performance results. The emphasis was on being positive in all settings, never critical. Don Burwell recalls that he used a hypothetical situation to kick off this training period:

> I explained to the group that the first thing that will happen when you say to them that you're aware you haven't done a good enough job in communicating with them about their performance and that you want to do a better job and need their help is that there'll be one guy out of every ten that will say "the heck with you, boss, I don't want to help." So we'd pick out one of the foremen in the group and say "Joe, how would you handle that kind of a situation?" The first reaction of most of the foremen was to resort to punishment—send him home for insubordination or reply "I'll give you a week's suspension,"—or "I'm gonna fire you." It was hard for them to get into the swing of responding in a positive fashion. But we role played the situation and they gradually began to understand what positive reinforcement was all about. The end result was usually something like "Okay, Joe, I need your help. I need you to change your mind and help me cause I can't make it without you, so I sure hope you will help."

This kind of extensive role playing and practice, in Burwell's view, was "critical" in launching the program. While it was difficult for the foremen to get into the new positive way of thinking, the total team of managers worked with them using the technique of role play to remove blocks about how to be positive. The experiment was launched as soon as the foremen who were to provide extrinsic reinforcement had been thoroughly trained. This was in the spring of 1974.

Burwell explained how the feedback sessions operated in practice:

> On Monday morning, the foremen of the six groups of thirty-seven employees who were on the "extrinsic only" feedback procedure would sit down with their groups and say: "Let me tell you how I saw you last week. I saw four of you in the range of "good" in this area of safety. I hope next week all five will be." He would never say anything about the person who was down on the bottom rung. Initially the group tended to say that they all five saw themselves

as just superior. You couldn't be any better. But gradually, over time, the groups began to accept the boss's evaluation. The boss would only praise the good employees, and say nothing about the ones who were substandard. But the one employee who was less than satisfactory on the chart would always know who he was. The group would also know.

Through these sessions a motivation to improve did develop, but not as a result of any direct criticism or negative feedback from the foreman.

A similar procedure was used with the group which received both intrinsic and extrinsic feedback. The foremen would feed back to the employees how they had evaluated themselves. He would say, for example, "Let me tell you how you said you saw yourselves last week." These self-evaluations were felt to have considerable accuracy, based upon a comparison of the average anonymous self-evaluations and performance of the total department.

There was an unexpected side effect of the intrinsic self-feedback approach. After thirty-five days the union filed a grievance against the company. They had three basic objections.

1) By evaluating their own performance the people were being asked to do the foreman's job.
2) It is unfair to ask people to write down how well they think they are performing and give it to the boss.
3) The boss does not give the people his evaluation of how well they are doing.

The company responded that the procedure forces the foremen to listen to the employees. They also pointed out that it was only an experimental activity. Eventually, the union agreed to go along with it for the period of the experiment.

Don Burwell feels that this experience and the grievance highlights a basic lesson with regard to human beings at work:

Where there is an absence of "How well am I doing, boss?" information, the grievance procedure in industry is usually the vehicle to get that information. But grievances are not seen as positive by most managers; they're seen as negative. The real essence of the situation is that human beings need to have some idea as to how well they are doing, and they can't always get it from the work itself or from internal awareness. They have to have some feedback from their superior. It turns out to be a basic psychological need.

So, from a practical point of view, the intrinsic self-initiated feedback process is not a practical alternative.

The results of the experiment were evaluated after thirty, sixty, and ninety days against baseline measures of the performance indicators collected before the experiment started. None of the four groups showed any changes in the attendance measure and absenteeism in all of these groups was relatively low.

On the other three performance indicators of cost, service, and safety, however, there were significant improvements over the ninety-day period in all four groups. The one exception was for costs in the control group which did not receive any feedback. This was the only performance decline over the ninety-day period, and this was the only group which failed to meet the cost objectives of 0.98 at the end of the experiment.

The general trend of the results, however, was for all four of the groups to improve in performance over the ninety days on the service, safety, and cost measures. Don Burwell outlines his view of the results achieved:

The group which received both intrinsic and extrinsic feedback had been the poorest in the year before. For thirty days, they made the most remarkable change; after sixty days there had been considerable change, and at the end of ninety days they were the top performer for the area on practically all of the criteria. It was a profound turnaround. The experimental group which received only extrinsic feedback from the supervisor was the second improving group, right on the heels of the other group. The third group, which received self-feedback, trended up in the first thirty days but then leveled off through the sixtieth day. Although the control group did show improvement on the service and safety measures, on an overall basis the trends were less significant than for the three groups which had a formal feedback program.

Burwell sees the results as extremely positive and likens them to a "productivity gold mine." He outlined his view of what seemed to be going on:

In your lower levels in worker groups—the people who really get the results—when the worker can know what the goals are without any question or doubt, and know when he has achieved, and periodically get reinforced when his boss says "super" or "excellent," that's the strongest thing a corporation, a firm, a business, or any operation can have going for it. And that is having its troops—the Indians if you will—knowing when they have met the goal.

Accordingly, Michigan Bell has taken steps to institute programs like the one just described on a regular basis. After ninety days, Burwell and his managers met and reviewed everything that had happened. This review was particularly welcomed by the manager of the control groups. He had become progressively more uneasy during the course of the experiment. Whereas he had been evaluated as "superior" before the experiment, now during the ninety-day experiment, he saw his peers catching up with him. He was very relieved when he saw the nature of the experimental design and understood the reasons.

The managers as a group worked out a continuing program to implement positive reinforcement. All of them decided that they wanted a combined approach of intrinsic plus extrinsic feedback. They felt that goal setting and feedback should be no less frequent than once a month. They also agreed that feedback should be as frequent as necessary so that those employees who were in trouble would have a basis for improvement.

The program was implemented in all of the groups. Within forty-five more days, according to Burwell, the manager of the control group was "just about back on top again. After six months on the new system, the achievement results were just profound. They were very excellent. At the end of the year the division had met four of its six objectives." (Two new objectives had been added to the original four: subjective evaluations of worker cooperation and of supervisor cooperation.)

At the end of the year the managers met and established higher objectives for the coming year. Then, during 1975, there was another

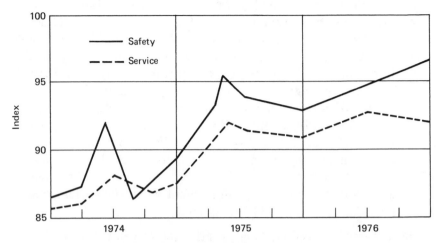

Fig. 4-1. Safety and service performance; combined district indices.

significant burst of improvement activity until the objectives were met, and the gains continued into 1976 (see Fig. 4-1).

In view of this evidence of success it is interesting that this approach has not been picked up by other areas of the Bell System, or even by other districts of Michigan Bell. Burwell points to several reasons for this. First of all, this type of program takes a great deal of attention by the superintendent, and not all managers are that knowledgeable about positive reinforcement methods or that dedicated. There is, as in most organizations, a degree of NIH—not invented here—philosophy which tends to inhibit the spread of the method. Finally, the general management at the headquarters of Michigan Bell has changed significantly over recent years, and in Burwell's estimation, they are not too familiar with the program and its operation. So there is not a great deal of press to spread it to other parts of the organization.

Burwell points to some cautions which have to be borne in mind if one plans to move a program like this into other areas:

These results tend to become the norm, the objective, and they are higher than the "superior" category in other areas of the business. In our group, excellent performance has become the norm. That doesn't allow a great deal of motivational reinforcement, because we weren't always as good as we are now. It took three years to get there, and that certainly could frighten the areas who were being put onto a program like this for the first time. They might feel that they have to all of a sudden go from an 83 to 98 percent. We didn't do that. It would be a big mistake to say: "Look what you've been missing; you go do it and get that 98." That's not what positive reinforcement is all about. You must understand what positive reinforcement is. It merely means that when they hit the target, give praise. And on a yearly basis, look at the targets and adjust them as appropriate. The targets will gradually escalate, because performance will continue to go up as people have clear-cut goals and get positive reinforcement when they attain them. For me, it is, in fact, a productivity gold mine.

The program of feedback and positive reinforcement at Michigan Bell is similar to what was done in the midwestern diecasting company, but more extensive. It very explicitly incorporates the process of goal setting. And it attempted to test the relative effectiveness of extrinsic as opposed to intrinsic feedback about performance. Although the changes were only relatively loosely controlled in the experimental sense, in combination they clearly have been effective in increasing the performance of the Buildings, Supplies, and Motor Equipment Division in the Metropolitan North area of Michigan Bell Telephone Company. The key seems to be:

1. Regular and timely feedback about performance provided by the supervisor.
2. An active process of setting goals to maintain performance or to improve it.
3. Positive reinforcement or praise for meeting goals and improving performance.

Again, as in the diecasting case, a component of more open communications between the supervisor and employees through the feedback and goal-setting process is implicit in the case. The approach clearly has applicability in a variety of organizations which wish to tap on the "gold mine" that Don Burwell has found at Michigan Bell.

5

Extending Research Findings from the Psychological Laboratory to the Field Setting

The Application of Goal Setting and Reinforcement Principles for Improving Productivity in the Wood-Products Industry*

Characteristically, in the behavioral sciences, there has been a considerable gap between theory and application. People concerned with theory have tended to conduct research with the sole objective of testing the validity of a theoretical statement and/or providing data which can be used to expand upon or qualify the theory. Usually there has been little direct concern with translating the theory into applications which organizations can use to enhance their performance effectiveness.

*Latham, G. P. and Baldes, J. J., The "practical significance" of Locke's theory of goal setting. *J. Appl. Psychol.* **60**: 122-124 (1975).

Latham, G. P. and Kinne, S. B., III, Improving job performance through training in goal setting. *J. Appl. Psychol.* **59**: 187-191 (1974).

Latham, G. P. and Yukl, G. A., Assigned versus participative goal setting with educated and uneducated woods workers. *J. Appl. Psychol.* **60**: 299-302 (1975).

Latham, G. P. and Yukl, G. A., Effects of assigned and participative goal setting on performance and job satisfaction. *J. Appl. Psychol.* **61**: 166-171 (1976).

Latham, G. P., Mitchell, T. R., and Dossett, D. L., Importance of participative goal setting and anticipated rewards on goal difficulty and job performance. *J. Appl. Psychol.* **63**: 163-171 (1978).

Latham, G. P. and Dossett, D. L., Designing incentive plans for unionized employees: A comparison of continuous and variable ratio reinforcement schedules. *Personnel Psychol.* **31**: 47-61 (1978).

Such theory-oriented research has usually dealt with relatively limited and abstract issues and has entailed complex experimental designs which are difficult, if not impossible, to duplicate in the real world. This research has often used subjects for the experiments who bear little resemblance to employees in working environments. Most notably, for example, theoretical research in psychology has placed an inordinate amount of emphasis upon the laboratory behavior of the white rat and the behavior of the college sophomore.

Applied research in the behavioral sciences, on the other hand, has to a disturbing extent ignored theory. Much of this research may be characterized as ad hoc, simplistically designed, and not articulated as a program of research studies which build upon one another to provide generalizable insights about better ways of enhancing organizational effectiveness.

At the Weyerhaeuser Company in Tacoma, Washington, however, a significant program of behavioral science research has been going on which is designed to evaluate the application of some theories and principles developed in the psychological laboratory to field settings. This research program has had some important results, both in the extension of knowledge about behavior in organizations as well as insights into ways to significantly increase productivity in work groups. It is a rare example of a systematic program of interlocking studies and applied research—thoroughly grounded in theory—which focuses on solving organizational problems, increasing productivity, and at the same time contributing generalizable insights for future application.

The field research has followed two major lines of effort:

1. The application of goal-setting principles to enhance performance, largely patterned around the laboratory and theoretical work of E. A. Locke of the University of Maryland, and

2. Operant reinforcement of behavior, applying principles articulated by B. F. Skinner of Harvard.

Yukl, G. A. and Latham, G. P., Consequences of reinforcement schedules and incentive magnitudes for employee performance: Problems encountered in an industrial setting. *J. Appl. Psychol.* **60:** 294–298 (1975).

Yukl, G. A., Latham, G. P., and Pursell, E. D., The effectiveness of performance incentives under continuous and variable ratio schedules of reinforcement. *Personnel Psychol.* **29:** 221–231 (1976).

We shall describe some of this work at Weyerhaeuser and discuss its implications for the enhancement of productivity in organizations.

The studies have been carried out with a range of worker groups, including tree planters, sawyers who cut timber, truck drivers, typists, research and development scientists and engineers, and mountain beaver trappers. The diversity of occupations covered and the diversity of the workers on such factors as skill level, education, ethnic group, or geographical location add to the richness of this series of interlocking studies. Such diversity also increases the potential for generalizing from these results to the world of work in general.

Goal-setting theory as developed by E. A. Locke makes a number of relatively straightforward propositions about the relationship between the conscious goals or intentions which individuals have with regard to performing a task and the actual performance on the task. Locke's work was done primarily in the laboratory using students who did such tasks as arithmetic problems or brainstorming. The major outcomes from his program of research suggested, among other things:

1. Setting *specific* goals will result in higher performance on a task than will the process of adopting an attitude of "do my best" on the task.

2. Where the goals are accepted by the individual, the difficulty of the goal is directly related to the performance which is registered. In other words, difficult but attainable goals lead to higher performance than do easy goals.

3. Knowledge of results or feedback about how one does in the attainment of goals can have an impact on performance, but it appears to be only through the process of its use in giving the individual a basis for setting new goals for performance. Feedback in and of itself has little impact on performance; its role appears to be one of helping the individual set either explicit or implicit goals for performance.

4. Monetary incentives appear to operate, as well, largely as a foundation for a person to set difficult goals for performance

in order to achieve the incentives and less as a support for motivation in and of themselves.

5. The concept of participative management, which has received considerable attention in the behavioral sciences, probably also contains a large component of goal setting. By obtaining the participation of subordinates in the decision-making process, performance goals frequently are either explicitly or implicitly developed, and participation enhances the commitment to attain those goals. More importantly, participation appears to lead to higher goals being set than is the case when the goals are set unilaterally by a supervisor.

Some of these concepts from goal-setting theory will be familiar to people who have been involved with management by objectives (MBO) programs. MBO, which builds upon some of the concepts articulated by Peter Drucker, consists of a series of procedures to set objectives jointly between a manager and a subordinate and then to evaluate job performance against those objectives. There is little real theoretical basis for MBO, but it is a practice which has been adopted by many organizations, particularly among managerial or professional employees.

Goal-setting theory, however, makes explicit statements about the dynamics of how goal setting can have a positive impact upon performance. It places less emphasis on participation or feedback and more emphasis upon the difficulty level and the specificity of the goals which are set than is the case with management by objectives.

The researchers at Weyerhaeuser saw in goal-setting theory the potential for designing programs which could have a significant impact on productivity in several areas of the company's operations. So, they set out to conduct some experiments to test the theory in field settings. In the process, they gained some understanding of where goal setting is or is not appropriate, some idea of the conditions which determine its success, and some insights into the practical aspects of how it can best be implemented in different settings.

Not all of the findings from this program of research were clear. Not all were positive. But, in general, the findings do reinforce the basic theory and do provide some guidelines on how to implement goal setting to enhance productivity in various areas of the logging industry.

One of the early studies on goal setting was done among truck drivers in six logging operations in Oklahoma. Each of the operations consisted of six to ten individuals who were engaged in cutting down the tree, moving it to a loading dock and onto a truck, and then driving the truck to the mill where it was weighed and unloaded. The company found that many of the trucks were being loaded below their optimum capacity, which resulted in excess expense in moving the timber from the forest to the mill. Apparently, the drivers were excessively cautious in loading the trucks because they were apprehensive about exceeding the legal load limit and receiving a citation from the Highway Department. Typically, the trucks were running somewhere between 50 and 60 percent of capacity on most runs.

The company tried several approaches to try to correct the situation. First of all, they explained to the truckers why it was necessary to carry loads closer to the legal capacity, but nothing happened. Then, an effort was made to install scales on the trucks so that out in the woods they could actually measure how close to capacity they were loading. However, the scales broke in the rugged terrain. So, finally, the research psychologists at Weyerhaeuser suggested to the company that they try goal setting to motivate the truckers to load closer to capacity. The company agreed to try the goal-setting approach when they saw that their problem of underloading had not gone away.

Gary Latham, one of the Weyerhaeuser psychologists, recalls:

> Some of the managers thought that was the funniest and most naive thing they'd ever heard of. They couldn't conceive how that would motivate anybody to do anything, because there wasn't any money involved, no recognition, and they, the truck drivers, would get nothing out of it.

Working with management, it was decided that a goal of 94 percent truck net weight would be a difficult but attainable performance goal. The drivers were given a thorough explanation of the program. It was pointed out to them quite clearly that it was an experimental program, that they would not be required to make more truck runs per day than they currently did, and that there would be no negative consequences if performance declined at some point during the experiment. They also knew that there was no additional monetary reward involved and no special training would be required. The only change would be that rather than being asked to "do their best" in loading close to the truck's weight limit, they now would have a specific goal of trying to load at 94 percent.

After a three-month period in which base rate loading information was collected for thirty-six logging trucks in the six operations in Oklahoma, the specific goal of 94 percent of capacity was instituted. Immediately, in the first month, the loading increased from 60 percent of capacity to over 80 percent. Then, following a dip in the second month, the loading factor again tended to increase, leveling off around the 90 percent level. The trend in performance over a total twelve-month period is shown in Fig. 5-1. This high level of performance continued to be maintained even several years after the implementation of the initial experiment.

It is evident that the goal-setting approach had a dramatic impact on increasing the productivity of these truckers. But the drop in performance during the second month after the implementation of goal setting was curious, so the researchers interviewed a number of the truckers to try to determine the reason for this drop. It was clear from the interviews that the truckers were testing the commitment of management to see that there would be no retribution if performance dropped. When they found that there was no punishment, performance picked up again in the third month.

The increase in productivity shown in Fig. 5-1 is not a trivial matter at Weyerhaeuser. Company accountants have calculated that the cost of moving that additional amount of timber from the forest to the mill would have required roughly a quarter of a million dollars for purchasing additional trucks. This productivity saving does not include costs for additional fuel or drivers which would have been required to match that productivity rate at the previous level of truck loadings. So, instituting specific, difficult, and attainable goals appears to have had a dramatic payoff in productivity in this truck loading operation.

The dynamics of "how" goal setting was working and "why" included a number of things. The goal-setting process injected a cer-

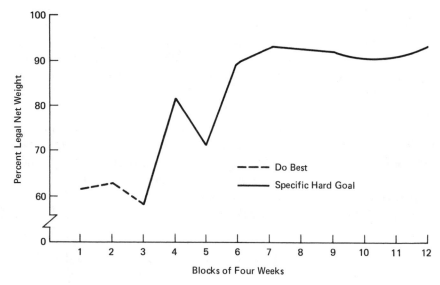

Fig. 5-1. Percent legal net weight of thirty-six logging trucks across blocks as a function of a specific hard goal.

tain amount of interest and challenge into what had previously been a relatively routine job. It became fun to try to meet or exceed the goal. There also was a certain amount of competition between the truckers, and one could hear them asking one another: "Hey, Joe, how did you do when you pulled into the wood yard last time?"

Meeting the goal became a matter of pride. A number of the truckers began to introduce minor modifications designed to help them in judging the weight of the load on the truck. Many began to keep informal records of their performance. In short, the goals provided a framework which injected some sport and challenge into the process of loading the trucks. This, along with the competition among the drivers, helped to maintain productivity at a high level during the period of the study and to continue after it was completed.

A second study of goal setting at Weyerhaeuser was undertaken among forty-eight crews involved in cutting trees in North Carolina and in Oklahoma and Arkansas. This study was designed to evaluate the differences between participatively set goals in which the individuals had a voice in what the goals should be versus goals that were assigned by the supervisor. Because there were large differences in the average educational level across the forty-eight logging work crews, it was also intended to test a hypothesis that the educational level of the work force would make a difference in terms of the appropriateness of participation in goal setting. Specifically, it was felt that participatively set goals would be more effective than assigned goals for a highly educated group (arbitrarily defined as having an education at the twelfth grade level or above) and that assigned goals would be more effective than participatively set goals for relatively uneducated work teams (less than nine years of education).

Each of the forty-eight work crews was assigned to one of three groups:

1. A group in which the supervisor assigned specific hard goals in terms of the number of "cunits" (100 cubic feet of wood) to be cut per week.
2. A "participative" group in which the men themselves set a specific production goal in terms of cunits each week.
3. A control group in which the sawyers were merely asked to "do your best" in terms of production.

Each of the sawyers was given a tally meter which he could use to keep track of the number of trees cut. The experiment ran for eight weeks.

There were some significant surprises when the results were analyzed. The trends were exactly opposite from those that had been hypothesized. Among the relatively low education crews, production was significantly higher when goals were set participatively than when they were assigned, and higher than they were under the "do your best" condition. Among the more educated crews, however, the three conditions did not differ significantly, though there was a tendency for higher productivity under assigned goals than under the participative condition or the "do your best" condition.

The researchers concluded that a number of factors besides education were probably impacting differential effectiveness of participative as opposed to assigned goals. For example, the uneducated crews tended to be in North Carolina. Conversely, the more educated crews tended to be concentrated in the Oklahoma/Arkansas region. Thus, other factors such as the nature of the terrain, climate, management, or experience could have impacted the results, rather than the simple factor of educational level.

But, the study did demonstrate that goal setting could have a significant impact on productivity (31 percent higher in the uneducated group with participatively set goals than under "do your best"). Similarly, for both the educated and uneducated groups, absenteeism was significantly lower under goal setting (both participative and assigned) than under the absence of goals. It was very clear that the process of setting specific, difficult, but attainable goals could have a significant positive impact on productivity. It was less clear under which conditions the goals should be set, participatively or assigned. So, additional research was undertaken to clarify that issue.

The next study was undertaken among typists in a word processing center. The study was in response to concern over productivity at the typing center. It involved forty-five female typists who worked in ten word processing centers, with three to six typists in each center.

For the experiment, the typists were assigned to either of two groups. In one group, goals for productivity were assigned by the supervisor. In the other group, goals were participatively set jointly by the typists and the supervisor. Goals were set each week and knowledge of the previous week's performance was helpful in setting the goals under both the participative and assigned conditions. Performance was measured by an index of the weighted sum of the number of lines typed during the week divided by the number of hours worked. The weights were determined based upon the difficulty level of the material being typed. The experiment ran for ten consecutive weeks.

The results are summarized in Fig. 5-2. After the ten weeks, both the typists in the groups for which goals were set participatively and those in the groups for which they were assigned were performing at a significantly higher rate of adjusted lines of typing per hour than before the experiment.

Productivity increased 18 percent for the participative group and 15 percent for the assigned group. Figure 5-2 also shows that in this particular experiment productivity did not increase significantly until

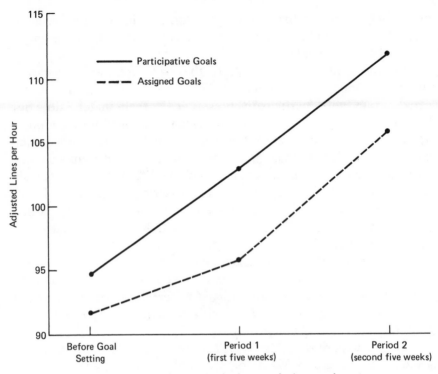

Fig. 5-2. Typing performance before and after goal setting.

the second five-week period. It was felt that a period of adjustment was needed for the goal setting to impact productivity and that some fear of a possible layoff, if productivity increased, had to dissipate before the significant results could be achieved. The process of participation in setting goals did not seem to be an important factor differentiating the performance improvement for this group of typists.

So, once again, with a very different category of employee, the researchers at Weyerhaeuser demonstrated that the process of setting specific, difficult, but attainable goals could have a significant impact on productivity. It was also shown that the impact could be achieved at no expense to the organization; no burdensome system of rewards or recognition was necessary and there was no real threat to the employees.

The final study in the area of goal setting was done among scientists and engineers in the research laboratory at Weyerhaeuser. In this study, seventy-nine engineers and scientists either participated in the setting of their performance goals or had them assigned. The goals were in terms of achieving a certain level of performance evaluated as "excellent" on a special evaluation procedure.

When the level of the goals set under participation as opposed to assigned conditions were compared, the participative group was found to have set significantly more difficult goals than those that were assigned by supervision. This suggested to the researcher that perhaps the positive effect of participation is primarily because of the level of difficulty which the workers themselves build into the goals that they set.

In the follow-up six months later to determine the levels of performance actually achieved by the scientists and engineers, both the group for which goals had been assigned and the participative group registered significantly higher levels of performance than a control group for which goals of "do your best" had been employed. Once again, specific, relatively difficult, but attainable goals had led to higher performance than the absence of such goals.

There was also a significant relationship between how difficult the goals were and the performance actually achieved. That is, people who set high goals tended in fact to register high levels of performance; individuals who set relatively easy goals performed less well. For this group of engineers and scientists, as was true in the word processing center, there were no significant differences in the actual performance obtained by individuals operating under assigned goals compared with individuals employing participatively set goals.

This program of research at Weyerhaeuser had demonstrated convincingly that the goal-setting theory as developed with college students in the psychological laboratory could have direct application in the field with a variety of employee types. It has been shown to be effective in increasing the productivity of truck drivers, loggers, research scientists, and typists. There are several common threads which seem to be in operation which make the process of setting goals effective:

1) First of all, by setting goals it is very often possible to clarify exactly what is expected of the individual. As one of the research

and development engineers stated, by receiving a specific goal from the supervisor he was able to "determine for the first time in fifteen years what that ——— really expected from me."

2) The process of working against explicit goals injects interest into the task. As Gary Latham points out in discussing the program of research at Weyerhaeuser:

Suddenly we're getting challenge, we're getting feedback, we're getting pride in performance. It's like bowling. The process of rolling a ball down an alley all day could be a pretty boring thing if we didn't turn it into a game and put some objectives on it in terms of getting a strike or a spare. I think that's all there is to a lot of this goal setting. It's a way of introducing meaning to a job. And there's an awful lot of jobs where you need meaning.

Now I'm not sure that it would work—say—on an assembly line. That's one of the things that we don't know; what are the limitations of goal setting? Where doesn't it work? Right now it's an art. I have a good feel for it, but I couldn't defend my feelings in a scientific forum. But so far, we're batting a thousand at Weyerhaeuser and I know goal setting works.

3) Several factors do appear to be important for the success of the goal-setting process. For one, there has to be some latitude for the individual to influence performance. That was the case with the sawyers, the truck drivers, the word processing typists, and certainly with the scientists and engineers. Where performance is rigidly controlled by technology or work flow, such as on the typical assembly line, goal setting probably will have little effect. Also it is important that the workers do not feel threatened with losing their jobs if they increase their performance under the goal-setting procedure. People have enough sense not to put themselves out of work by being too productive. In the jobs at Weyerhaeuser, this was not a problem as there was always "more to do" in the logging operations, typing centers, and R & D laboratories. But even in these studies, in the word processing center, there seemed to be a productivity lag tied largely to some concern about job insecurity.

4) Using participative approaches in setting goals appears to be at

least as effective as assigning goals, even though some of the studies did not demonstrate clear superiority.

At the very least, there is no evidence that assigned goals are superior to those that are participatively set. Therefore, based on the evidence so far, it would probably be wise to use participation in the goal-setting procedure.

Gary Latham feels that the series of field studies undertaken at Weyerhaeuser have adequately demonstrated the potential effectiveness of goal setting for yielding significant productivity increases.

When we got that quarter million dollar savings from the truckers, that's when people truly stopped being cynical about goal setting.

Not all the research at Weyerhaeuser to increase productivity has focused on goal setting. There has also been a series of significant studies on incentives—studies to determine what characteristics of the system of rewards will positively impact performance. Specifically, these studies have looked at monetary rewards for performance and ways in which these rewards may be administered to have a maximum impact on production.

Like the goal-setting research, these studies have been built upon psychological theory which developed from laboratory experimentation. In this case, the studies have been based upon principles of operant conditioning and reinforcement, most notably the work of B. F. Skinner at Harvard.

In simple terms, operant reinforcement theory rests upon the proposition that behavior is determined by its consequences. In the laboratory, it has been determined that a white rat will press a lever or a pigeon will peck at a target in a specified sequence if either animal is to receive a desired reward—a food pellet. Translating this principle into the area of monetary rewards in an organization, it should hold that money—or any valued reward—can and will increase the rate at which people will work if it is directly contingent upon their performance and if it is given immediately after the desired behavior occurs.

One line of research in this area has investigated the effects of various "schedules" of reinforcement. That is, are the effects different depending on whether the reward is given every time the desired behavior is exhibited, or if the reward is given upon some fixed schedule or interval such as every second time or every eighth time the behavior is exhibited. Alternately random variable schedules have also been investigated. In these cases, the desired behavior is reinforced randomly, but on the average of one out of every two times or one out of every eight times.

Laboratory research on different schedules of reinforcement has suggested that learning is best under continuous schedules of reinforcement, but that once the behavior has become learned, some variable intermittent schedule of reinforcement may maintain the behavior for a longer period and actually increase the response rate to a higher level than is the case with a continuous schedule. Presumably, over the long run, continuous reinforcement schedules lose their motivation potential and become "old hat."

There has been little or no research in industry looking at different schedules of reinforcement with monetary incentives. The program at Weyerhaeuser, which used monetary incentives, was thus a pioneering effort to assess the effectiveness of different reinforcement schedules to enhance productivity.

The first study was done among tree planters in North Carolina. The purpose was to test incentives for increasing productivity, and specifically, to test different reinforcement schedules. Tree planting can be a boring and difficult job. They dig a hole, plant a tree, go ten feet further down the row, dig another hole, plant a tree, etc. The planters work in pairs, and each pair can plant somewhere between 1,000 and 3,000 trees in a day. The trees are contained in bags of roughly 1,000 seedlings each. It was felt that an incentive program might inject some challenge into this task and relieve some of the boredom and monotony.

In the first study of the tree planting operations at Weyerhaeuser in North Carolina, the planting crews were primarily uneducated, black workers. They were randomly assigned to four groups:

Group A: A group of planters who were to receive continuous reinforcement for their production. For every bag of trees planted, each pair of planters was to receive two dollars as incentive payment, in addition to their prescribed hourly wages.

Group B: A group of planters who would receive a variable schedule of reinforcement. The schedule called for a pair to receive four dollars half of the time that they planted a full bag of trees *and* correctly guessed the results of a coin toss. Thus, on the average, they too would receive two dollars per bag, but it would be on a variable schedule of every other time, on the average.

Group C: A group that would receive a reinforcement on the average 25 percent of the time. In this group a pair of planters would receive eight dollars each time they planted a bag of trees *and* correctly guessed the result of *two* coin tosses. Again, over the long term they would average two dollars per bag of trees planted, but would receive it only 25 percent of the time in the form of an eight dollar bonus.

Group D: A control group, in which no incentive would be added.

Thus, the three incentive groups received, on the average, the same amount of money (two dollars for every bag planted), but the frequency with which it was received varied.

The program was explained to the people as follows:

We realize that your work can be difficult and tiring. As a result, we would like you to have a chance to earn more money and have some fun in the process. From here on in you are going to have the opportunity to receive four dollars (eight dollars) every time you plant a bag of trees. All you have to do is correctly guess the outcome of a coin toss (the outcome of two coin tosses). If you guess incorrectly, you don't really lose anything because you will always receive your regular hourly pay.

The study ran for fifteen weeks. By comparing the results, in terms of bags of trees planted per man-hour, for a three-week premeasurement period with a period of measurement after the incentives were instituted, it was found that:

1. For Group A, which received a continuous reinforcement of two dollars per bag every time a bag was planted, productivity increased by 33 percent.
2. For Group B, which received four dollars on the average 50 percent of the time for every bag planted, productivity *decreased* by 8 percent.
3. For Group C, which received eight dollars 25 percent of the time, productivity increased by 18 percent.

4. In the control group, there was essentially no change between the before and after measures of productivity.

The striking thing was that there was such a large increase in productivity—33 percent under continuous reinforcement. This was contrary to the trends one might have expected based upon prior laboratory work. And the fact that the four dollar increase on the average half of the time actually resulted in a decrease in productivity, was difficult to explain. However, it was clear that there were many confounding factors in the experiment which led to the somewhat ambiguous results.

For one thing, there was a considerable amount of misunderstanding of the program in the two groups which received variable schedules of reinforcement. This was particularly true in Group B in which there was a great deal of concern about the program as being a form of "gambling." There were many women in this group, and they were particularly negative to the gambling aspect. This was less true in Group C, which received eight dollars on the average of 25 percent of the time, though even here there was some concern by the supervisor, who was a part-time minister, about the gambling nature of the program.

There were other problems concerning the mechanics of administering the program, particularly under the variable schedules (such as the supervisor frequently dropping the coin in the swamp) which led the researchers to conclude that the actual experimental test of the differences between continuous and variable reinforcement schedules was not conclusive. But the fact that productivity could be increased under incentives, such as the 33 percent increase under continuous reinforcement, did suggest that productivity could be significantly impacted by adding incentives to the task. A follow-up study the next year again demonstrated an increase in productivity under a continuous reinforcement schedule. It remains for another test to determine more explicitly the value of different reinforcement schedules.

A third Weyerhaeuser study on incentives and schedules of reinforcement was carried out among mountain beaver trappers in the Northwest. The mountain beaver is a nocturnal rat with no tail. It resembles a woodchuck. The beaver lives in the side of a hill and devours young seedling trees. Therefore, timber companies attempt to control the mountain beaver through trapping it.

In 1975 at Weyerhaeuser, beaver trapping was found to be a very expensive operation. The cost, on the average, was $16.75 to trap one beaver. So, the company searched for ways to motivate their trappers so that they would learn to distinguish a "live" beaver hole from a bad one to increase their yield.

It was felt that job enrichment would not be effective because, as Gary Latham puts it, "It was just an extremely tough job; Mother Nature wouldn't allow a lot of job changes." Also there was some question as to whether goal setting would be appropriate because of the variability in the terrain and an inability to specify what would be a reasonably difficult but attainable goal in terms of the number of beavers trapped. Instead, the company decided to try incentives designed to increase the effort which the trapper put into the job and, more specifically, to encourage the trappers to learn more about the subtle indications and cues of where to set their traps for maximum yield. Since most of the trappers were highly motivated by money, the monetary incentive approach seemed reasonable.

As in the case of the tree planters, different schedules of reinforcement were tried. To avoid the ambiguity that occurred in the study of tree planters due to the concern over the "gambling" aspects of the incentive plan, they made sure that everyone fully understood the procedures and that the union supported the experiment. The trappers, who tended to be highly educated, some with college degrees, were randomly divided into two groups:

Group A: This group was assigned to a continuous reinforcement schedule for the first four weeks in which they received one dollar for every rat trapped. This incentive payment was in addition to their basic wages of five dollars per hour. Then, for the second four-week period, they received four dollars contingent upon trapping a rat and correctly guessing the color of one out of four marbles which they drew from a bag held by the supervisor.

Group B: In this group the procedure was reversed. For the first four weeks they operated under a variable reinforcement schedule of 25 percent and then for the last four weeks of the experiment under a continuous reinforcement schedule receiving one dollar for every beaver trapped. The money was paid immediately by the supervisor when the trappers brought the rat to a central location. Payment was in cash using one dollar bills.

The experiment ran for eight weeks. The results were dramatic. There was a 41 percent increase over the eight-week period in the number of beavers trapped per man-hour in the field. Production rose from an average of 0.44 beavers per hour before the experiment to 0.63 beavers per hour after the incentives were applied. Other productivity measures also showed significant increases over the eight-week period. There was a 23 percent increase in the number of beavers trapped per acre and there was an 11 percent increase in the number of acres covered by the trappers per man-day. These productivity increases resulted in dramatic reductions in the cost of trapping a rat. The cost dropped from an average of $16.75 per rat before the experiment to $12.86—a 23 percent reduction, even with the additional cost of the incentive payment. Over the total eight weeks, fourteen trappers caught 2,006 beavers at a net savings of $7,703, not counting the savings from reduced tree replanting costs. It is quite evident that instituting financial incentives into this particular job resulted in significant productivity increases and cost reductions for Weyerhauser.

The study yielded some interesting results with regard to the comparison of continuous and variable reinforcement schedules. On an overall average, trappers under the continuous schedule produced more than when they were under a variable schedule—by 16 percent. As Fig. 5-3 shows, both groups were at the same level of production initially, but Group B, which changed from a variable to a continuous schedule, increased its production by 45 percent over the course of the experiment, whereas Group A which changed from a continuous to a variable reinforcement schedule increased by only 25 percent.

The fact that both groups increased their production suggests that there was considerable learning going on about how to trap the beavers effectively. Interviews with the trappers tended to substantiate this and revealed that the trappers were learning how to recognize subtle cues about which holes were "live."

In view of this evident learning effect, a hypothesis was formulated—

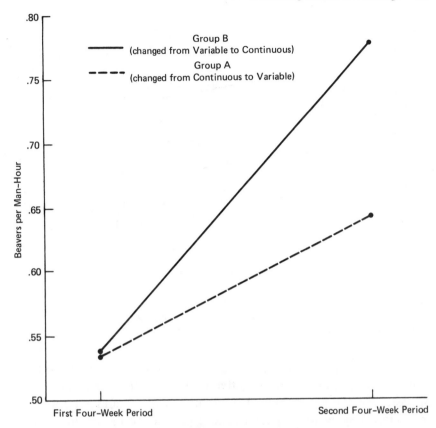

Fig. 5-3. Trapping productivity under continuous and variable reinforcement.

based upon suggestions from laboratory research on operant reinforcement—that continuous reinforcement would be most supportive of learning among trappers who were relatively inexperienced and that for those who had already learned the trapping job, variable reinforcement would be more motivating and therefore would result in higher performance. To test this hypothesis, the sample of trappers was divided in terms of their level of experience with mountain beaver trapping.

As Fig. 5-4 shows, the hypothesis was confirmed. Those trappers who were characterized as being relatively inexperienced or low on trapping ability had 11 percent higher productivity under the continuous reinforcement schedule than they did under the variable

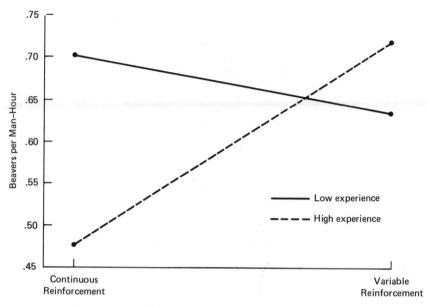

Fig. 5-4. Productivity of experienced and inexperienced trappers under variable and continuous reinforcement.

schedule. Presumably, the continuous schedule helped them to learn how to do the job more effectively. The results were exactly the opposite for the group judged to be high in ability and experience as trappers. They were 51 percent more productive under the variable reinforcement schedule than they were under the continuous schedule. While the number of trappers involved is relatively small in this analysis, the trends do suggest how different schedules of reinforcement may be more effective for some groups of workers than for others. The extent to which the task has been learned if the worker has a high level of ability seems to be a key factor to consider.

On balance, this program of incentives has clearly been a resounding success in increasing productivity in this segment of Weyerhaeuser. Interviews with a number of the supervisors and trappers indicate that part of the reason for its success is that it injects some excitement and fun into what ordinarily is a rather boring and difficult job. As one trapper says:

It builds our interest over and beyond our regular day-to-day type thing. We're making more money than we thought we would. The traps are going in a heck of a lot better. We're covering the ground better. It has really upped our productivity.

When asked about the issue of gambling, another replies:

There is no gambling issue. Guys really get psyched out by it, man. They like it. It adds something to it. There is real excitement. The guys who are on the continuous schedule all stand around and cheer for the guys on the variable schedule when they're pulling the marble. It's really great. It's not gambling; we aren't using our own money. It isn't as if we would lose anything. We always get our hourly wage regardless. We don't see the connection with gambling.

And the supervisors saw a high level of interest in the program and felt that employees were really excited about it.

They are much more willing to go to work. They really get into the more difficult areas now. I've seen an increase in productivity. The guys are gung-ho. I'd rate the enthusiasm eight on a ten point scale. Wait 'til you see them shaking for those marbles. Boy do they get excited—especially on the days we pull the traps. This program is going way better than I had anticipated.

A member of a variable crew expresses this excitement:

It really adds a lot to the program. Excitement. The heartbeat really gets going. You should see the sweat on a man's forehead when he's trying to pick the right marble. Trying to get all the dollars he can.

And a supervisor comments on how the employees feel when they select the wrong marble under the variable reinforcement schedule:

The men are disappointed; they go back and even try harder to catch more rats so that they can get more shots at the marble. You get a much better response and excitement from these people than you do the workers on a continuous schedule. The variable schedule is a big deal. Everyone stands around and roots for the guy when he picks the marble. It is great!

The incentive is seen as a nice little additional bonus which many of the trappers like, because:

You don't have to tell your wife about the money. It's money that disappears in your pocket.

The biggest criticism of the program on the part of management was that the incentive program was turning into a "circus." Gary Latham comments:

They're absolutely right. That's exactly what we're trying to do. It's a crummy job, and we're trying to turn it into a circus. How many circuses have trouble drawing a crowd? This will decrease the attendance problem as well as increasing productivity.

The results of this small experiment seem to bear him out, as did a follow-up study the next year in which comparable results were obtained. Clearly, monetary reinforcement for production in mountain beaver trapping has had a big positive return to the company. And, clearly, there are principles learned from this experiment which can be applied to other jobs throughout the company.

What does the Weyerhaeuser experience suggest to organizations which are interested in increasing their productivity by better human resource utilization? The answer is simple. Both goal setting and the use of reinforcements and rewards for desired performance can be powerful devices to increase production. And these two approaches can supplement and build upon one another, if carefully applied in the right situation.

By setting performance goals, a supervisor can clarify what is expected of an employee and build considerable interest into jobs which under many circumstances might be considered mundane and unmotivating. The key ingredients of an effective goal-setting process are:

1. The goals which are set must deal with specific and tangible aspects of the employee's behavior in which effective performance is easily identifiable, and not with vague generalities.
2. The goals must cover aspects of an employee's behavior over which the employee has some control and latitude to act.
3. The goals that are set should be relatively difficult but attainable.
4. The employee should be asked to participate in setting the goals, if at all possible.
5. Finally, the employee's job security must not be threatened if the goals are attained.

An organization which is interested in trying the goal-setting procedure to enhance productivity can search for jobs which reflect these conditions. In most organizations, there are many jobs where systematic goal setting has a tremendous potential for significant increases in productivity. And there are many other jobs where, by minor modifications in procedures or organization, these positive potentials can be built in.

Many organizations may also obtain productivity increases through a program of behavioral reinforcement. Again, these activities must be carried out in job settings where the employee has the potential for increasing productivity, where he or she is not threatened with loss of job security if productivity does increase, and where the rewards to be used for reinforcement purposes are valued by the employees. There are several key points to an effective behavioral reinforcement program:

1. The reward must be directly contingent upon the employee performing in the desired fashion. That is, the reward should be for planting the bag of trees, catching the beaver, etc.
2. The employee must understand the desired behavior which will be rewarded—what she or he has to do to get the reinforcement. The role of goal setting here to clarify expectations can be very useful.
3. The reinforcer or reward must consist of something which is valued by the employee and it must be given in a large enough quantity to be meaningful. We tend to think of money—because most people do value money—but there are many other potential reinforcers which should be considered. These can consist of tangible things such as time off to attend some special program or for personal use, or more intangible things such as recognition or praise.
4. A continuous reinforcement schedule—reinforcement each time the behavior is exhibited—probably should be employed when the employee is learning the task. Praise each correct response in the training session; pay a bonus for each unit produced; and so forth.
5. A variable reinforcement schedule may be useful for injecting excitement and motivation once the task has been learned. The

employee must understand and accept the variable procedure, however, for it to be effective.

In most organizations there are many jobs where the systematic use of reinforcement, such as we have described here, can have real and lasting effects on productivity. It merely takes a little bit of imagination and daring and a willingness to try something different to find those positions and to test the power of these potentially important tools for enhancing productivity.

Interim Summary For Chapters 2–5 Illustrating Behavioral Change Efforts

The studies that we have dealt with so far in four very different organizations illustrate the application of behavioral approaches to enhancing performance in organizations. They draw upon what may loosely be termed "operant conditioning principles" derived from basic research in the psychological laboratory. The thrust of these principles is that behavior is a function of its consequences. For every behavior in an organizational setting, whether it be high levels of productivity, absenteeism, or quality workmanship, there are a variety of consequences for the individual some of which are positive and some of which should be viewed as negative. The operant approach tries to maximize the positive consequences for desired behavior—high productivity, high quality, good attendance, etc.—to provide a system in which these outcomes are clearly contingent upon the desired behavior, and to be sure that the desired behaviors are rewarded or reinforced.

In operational terms, this usually entails: 1) some process of *goal-setting*, so that the desired behavior is clarified and the individual understands what he or she has to do in order to receive the reward or reinforcement; 2) a process of *feedback*, so that the individual is aware of when the goals have been achieved and has a basis for setting new goals; and 3) actually providing positively valued *reinforcements* or rewards for meeting the goals. Reinforcement may be intrinsic—inherent in the very process of meeting the goals—as appeared to be the case with the loggers loading trucks in Oklahoma. Or, rewards may be in the form of an extrinsic reinforcer, such as the monetary incentive for attendance in the bakery of the supermarket distribution center or among the mountain beaver trappers and tree planters. In each of these cases, there was a direct monetary reward associated with obtaining the desired objectives. Finally, reinforcement may be less tangible, taking the form of praise and encouragement by supervisors, as was the case in the Michigan Bell application of operant conditioning principles and in the midwestern diecasting company.

Such behavioral approaches to shaping behavior and enhancing performance do not operate in a vacuum. They usually have components of other principles and practices associated with the effective utilization of human resources which supplement and enhance the behavioral strategies. In the cases which we have presented, there was frequently an element of participation or involvement on the part of the employees. This was explicitly structured into some of the experiments in Weyerhaeuser where participatively set goals were contrasted with assigned goals. While the experimental results were not always clear-cut, at the very least, participation did not have a negative effect in any of the experiments. The communication involved when supervisors work with employees to set goals, as in the diecasting case or the Michigan Bell case, clearly enhances the employees' involvement and acceptance of the goals and heightens their motivation. In several of the cases, as well, there was a large component of injecting "fun" into the job setting. The poker game incentive for attendance brought excitement to what otherwise was a relatively routine work setting. And the use of continuous and variable schedules of reinforcement in the lumbering industry turned relatively nasty and difficult jobs into jobs with a certain amount of excitement and enjoyment. Rather than turning the work situation into a "circus," such strategies are perfectly legitimate approaches for enhancing job involvement and motivation. They clearly support the application of behavioral principles of goal setting, feedback, and positive reinforcement which these cases have demonstrated can have a powerful potential for enhancing productivity in a variety of organizations.

6
Building a Participative Management System to Enhance Product Quality*

In the aerospace industry, perhaps the most critical component of productivity is quality. On a combat mission or on an astronaut's trip to the moon, there is little margin for unreliability in the electronic, electrical, or mechanical devices which support the flight. This overriding concern was directly behind a comprehensive program to initiate a system of participative management at a large aerospace company in California during the late 1960s. We shall use the pseudonym "Spacetronics" for the name of this company.

Spacetronics was the primary supplier of the electronics—principally airborne computers—required for the guidance system of Minuteman ICBMs, the mainstay of the United States' strategic missile arsenal. Dr. Frank Connelly, a psychologist concerned with human factors design at Spacetronics, summarizes how the program started:

> It was quite simple. If a whole missile can get lost because of a wiring problem, you know you have a quality assurance concern. Our original approach was to attack that concern using human factors techniques. But at Spacetronics, it became clear that the problems we were having were motivational problems, not human factors. The more we talked with people, the more evident it became that there were problems in setting goals, in feedback about performance, and in general communications with supervision. So we started to focus on these issues, rather than the hardware side of product quality.

*Chaney, F. B. and Teel, K. S., Participative management—A practical experience. *Personnel*, pp. 8–19 (Nov./Dec. 1972).

So the Human Factors Group at Spacetronics went to Jim Garber, Director of Manufacturing, suggesting a different approach to enhance motivation which was built around participative management. The objective was, first of all, to build employee commitment to the goals of the organization—goals of high productivity and overall high quality. Secondly, a participative management system hopefully would provide a means to get employees involved in identifying and solving problems; to bring to bear their intimate familiarity with the everyday work in order to identify the problems they faced daily and to help overcome them.

Jim Garber agreed with the program as outlined by the human factors psychologists. He recognized a great need for quality improvements and high levels of reliability in the Minuteman program and saw that there was a potential to improve. And he also agreed with the philosophy of starting from the bottom to identify problems and to begin to solve them.

Two pilot studies were undertaken to develop a method for fostering a participative style. One study was in an electronic inspection department and the other study was in a manufacturing department. In the inspection department, the pilot study contrasted the effectiveness of goals set individually with employees versus goals set in group settings in reducing inspection paperwork errors. Such errors were excessive and causing delays in shipment of the end product, and thus it was important to reduce them.

For the pilot study, supervisors of two equivalent groups received six hours of training in concepts of employee motivation and performance improvement. This training was supplemented by one hour of direct counseling by a staff psychologist on group and individual concepts of setting goals.

One of the supervisors met with his employees as a group for one hour per week over a four-week period and worked with them to set goals for reducing paperwork errors. The other supervisor met individually with his inspectors on a number of short occasions over the four weeks to set individual goals for reducing errors. Both supervisors set the goal of a 50 percent reduction in errors.

Over a three-month evaluation period the group for which improvement goals had been set as a group actually obtained a 75 percent reduction in errors. At the same time, there was no significant improvement in the other group in which goals were set individually.

These positive results plus the preferences of the supervisors led Spacetronics to decide to use group-set goals in subsequent programs. First of all, the group goal-setting procedure was more efficient and took up less supervisory time. It also built group communications and shared objectives. And the experience showed that in the final analysis it was really not possible to make a clear distinction between group and individual goals since most employees wanted to know how their own performance compared with the department as a whole before committing themselves to individual performance goals. So, in effect, goals were being set on a group basis, but without the benefit of the group communication and sense of sharing. In addition, it was important to use the group for problem solving and as a base for setting performance goals, and this was lost, by and large, in the individual sessions.

A second pilot study was carried out using five groups involved in manufacturing computer components for the Minuteman missiles. The five supervisors in these assembly operations were given extensive training in an eight-hour course spread over seven weekly sessions. The training involved an orientation to participative management techniques and goal setting, principles of performance measurement, concepts of communication and motivation, procedures for goal setting and establishing feedback, and group discussion techniques. The supervisors then met with their employees in a number of sessions to apply the participative management techniques and group goal-setting procedures. Staff psychologists attended these meetings and immediately following the meetings provided counseling and feedback to the supervisors about their performance.

By and large, the results of these pilot projects were highly successful, though they illustrate some of the problems of evaluating a program like this in an ongoing organization. In two of the five groups, significant changes occurred either in the work assignments or in personnel which made it impossible to assign specific goals to the groups or to obtain reliable performance data. In both of these cases, however, the supervisors were relatively positive to the process even though it was not possible to evaluate it conclusively.

In the other three groups, however, there were significant positive results. For example, production and quality goals were established during a series of four weekly meetings in a group consisting of five cable assembly operators. These sessions also resulted in suggestions for changes in tooling and clarification of job responsibilities. Over an eight-week period, production in this group increased from an average of twelve cables per week to 16.5 cables—a 38 percent productivity improvement. Quality improved from 0.8 defects per cable to less than 0.3 defects per cable in the latter period of the study—an improvement of 63 percent.

In another group involved with assembling circuit boards, the group session resulted in some significant changes in the way the job was designed. This actually was a job enrichment change. Formerly, the work in the department was organized in two assembly lines with each person doing a part of the work. The group suggested a unit build approach in which each person completed the total circuit board. This change was implemented, and the average time to assemble a board was reduced from 5.5 hours to 4.2 hours—a reduction of 24 percent. In addition, quality improved as a result of the individualized feedback given to each operator about errors and the operator's responsibility to perform his or her own rework. This reduced the defect rate by 50 percent.

In another group, which consisted of eleven operators and a lead woman performing most of the work on a nine-position stationized line with three additional stations for checking, rework, and installation of shortage items, in a series of four meetings the group arrived at goals to significantly reduce the number of defects per board. In addition, they discussed problems which were impacting the production and ways of solving the problems, as well as goals for increasing production. Based on an average level of 1.5 defects per board, the group established a goal of 0.5 defects. Two months after the goal was set the defect rate was 0.6 per board—an improvement of 60 percent.

On the production side, the stable output had been twenty-five boards per week. The group of supervisors established an output goal of fifty acceptable boards per week. After nine weeks, the group attained an average of forty boards per week. After five months a level of fifty boards was attained—an improvement of 100 percent. In terms of production costs, the average assembly time per system of five boards was reduced from 110 to 40 hours—a reduction of 55 percent resulting in a direct cost saving of $25,000 during the six-month period following the problem-solving and goal-setting process.

In this instance, as in the others, it is important to recognize that while participation in goal setting can result in significant productivity improvements, the process of participation also helps by identifying, clarifying, and gaining a commitment to solve the problems which are getting in the way of the production process. The shared commitment to do things more efficiently is an important component leading to the kinds of productivity increases attained in these pilot projects at Spacetronics.

Following these significant demonstrations of the potential gains to be attained from such a system of participative management, Jim Garber recalls how George Carson—the factory manager— "grabbed the program and ran with it." Jim Garber provided full support for this process of vigorous and extensive application of the concepts throughout the organization.

George recalls: "Well, I believed in it. The first-level supervisor is key to the whole program. So we went right to them to make it work, sometimes even going around the other levels of management."

George recalls how they decided that they "needed a person dedicated to the program—somebody who has the sole responsibility to make it work. We used Dr. Harry Baker from the University very extensively as we pushed the program more."

Baker recalls how initially the major focus was on training.

> We gave supervisors eight to twelve hours of training, but it really wasn't too worthwhile. We discussed motivation theory a la Maslow, discussion techniques à la Maier, and so forth. But the supervisors were so handicapped in trying to apply all this stuff. They got so bogged down that nothing happened.

So Baker began to move out more directly to help them.

The initial thrust to implementing participative management was on the goal-setting and feedback process. But the supervisors varied tremendously in their willingness and ability to implement the concepts. Some said, "What goal do you want to hit?" Others said, "Here's the goal, how can we reach it?" The latter approach seemed to work better, in Baker's experience.

Experience in two electronic module assembly groups illustrates the differences between supervisors in their ability and willingness to implement the concept. Both groups performed essentially the same type of work and both supervisors had received the same training on how to use group techniques. However, it was very evident that one supervisor was successful in obtaining a very high level of group participation while the other obtained little, if any, group participation. In the low participation group, the supervisor tended to be defensive in meetings and to discourage employee participation by his lack of interest in the problems and the solutions raised by employees. Over several months the number of modules produced per unit of time in the high participation group increased significantly, while production in the low participation group did not change. The supervisor of the low participation group stopped collecting data at the end of the fourth two-week period—in effect he withdrew himself from the project.

Recognizing such individual differences in willingness and ability to implement participative techniques, Baker changed his orientation from one of "give a training program" to one of "go out and help them." His orientation was, "You are the experts, and we're here to help." He served as an auditor and a catalyst to make good group leaders out of the supervisors.

In addition to setting goals, an important component of the approach which they pushed involved feedback. Feedback was always given each week on Monday, and sometimes more often. Feedback was given orally by the supervisor, though many of the production lines also had charts showing performance and these were posted at the head of the line. Sometimes the goal would be reset at the feedback sessions and if so they were usually modified upward.

As the concept gained more acceptance under the vigorous encouragement of George Carson, it began to cover all types of work involved at Spacetronics: planning, machine shop, light assembly, computer boards, shipping, etc. Overall, some 3,000 people eventually were involved representing 25 to 30 percent of the organization.

An example of how the process worked is illustrated by a department which manufactured read and write heads for computers. Production had been running at the rate of 300 acceptable read heads per week. The department was falling behind in meeting the requirements for the Minuteman guidance computers and needed close to 600 heads per week to get on a catch-back schedule. In the goal-setting process, the supervisor told employees "We need 600 a week;

how are we going to get there?" The group worked participatively to develop a plan for meeting that requirement, and production rose to 800 acceptable parts per week. By soliciting employee participation in solving the production problem, dramatic results were achieved.

Harry Baker recalls that one area of constant friction in the manufacturing environment was between quality assurance and production. The participative approach was used to get the inspectors and the production people together into a total group so that they could develop shared goals and objectives. Baker found that when this was done skillfully, the quality inspectors tended to put production as their first priority and the production personnel began to focus more on quality. Immediate feedback regarding the results achieved, both in quality and in production, built a strong sense of commitment by both groups to achieve the overall performance objectives.

Experience in other instances showed how participation had to be engaged in actively for positive results to be achieved. For example, in one group of women there was the suggestion to have music in the work area. Some tapes were prepared and earphones given to members of the group, and production increased significantly. It was then decided to provide music to everyone in the department, since the results had been so positive. However, it did not work. There was no impact on production in the other groups. The active involvement of employees in the decision was the crucial missing component.

In another situation there were three work groups using ten-power scopes as part of their assembly process. One group complained that they were facing a bare wall and that they would prefer to have their benches turned around so that they would have more awareness of the rest of the manufacturing area. Management concurred and turned the benches around for all three groups. It was found that the group that wanted the benches turned was very pleased by the change; the others were just indifferent. Again, the degree of participation in the decision seemed to be the key factor.

One area of initial concern dealt with the reactions that the union would have to this system of participative management. Baker recalls:

Everybody was worried, but there really wasn't any problem. I remember one representative who came up to me and said: "I don't know what you're doing, but you've relieved me of all the little nasty grievances. Now if there's a grievance, it's a real one. Not some of the picky little things that we used to get before." We had no difficulty with the union.

A summary evaluation of the results achieved was provided by six departments in the Minuteman manufacturing area and a control department which was not involved in the program. The six departments were rated independently by two psychologists in terms of the degree of participative management that actually was employed. There was almost perfect agreement between the two raters. Based upon the composite of their evaluations, two of the groups were designated as low participation, two as medium, and two as high. Figure 6-1 shows the percent change in performance over the period of the program for these six groups and the control group, as well as the percent favorable evaluations registered on an attitude survey.

It is clear from Fig. 6-1 that there is a significant relationship between the degree of participation and both the degree of favorable job attitudes and the degree of production improvements. Favorable job attitudes range from 35 percent in the groups with no participation to 80 percent where there are high levels of participation. In terms of performance, an average of 45 percent was obtained in the medium participation groups and 90 percent in the high participation

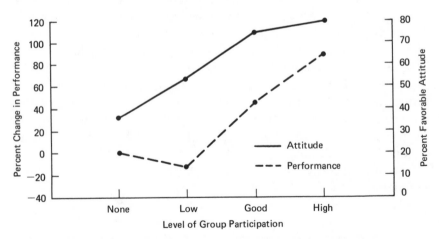

Fig. 6-1. Impact of group participation on production performance and employee attitude.

groups, while there was no significant change in the low participation groups or in the control group which was not involved in the program. The trends strongly support the conclusion that the degree of effective group participation is an important component of increases in performance and also in favorable job-related attitudes.

On an overall basis, over four years quantitative performance data were collected for forty groups involved in the participative program at Spacetronics. Of these, twenty-seven groups showed statistically significant performance gains, twelve showed no significant changes, and one showed a significant decline. Of the twenty-seven groups where significant improvements were registered, production increases averaged 20 to 30 percent along with 30 to 50 percent decreases in errors. The results in terms of job attitudes were also positive. On an overall basis the program seems clearly to have been successful. As George Carson puts it: "It paid off. There's no doubt in my mind."

In the face of this evident success, why is it that this approach for active implementation of participative management is no longer used. The reasons may be directly attributed to the downturn in the Minuteman program and the roller coaster manpower practices so prevalent in the aerospace industry. In a short period of time, manpower in Spacetronics dropped from 30,000 to around 10,000. Because of the bumping clause in the union contract and the general disruption of the downturn, most of the teams were broken up. Also, the management which had been supporting the program were either transferred or replaced; a new president was installed, Jim Garber was transferred to the East Coast, Harry Baker was no longer retained as a consultant. Frank Connelly summarized the situation:

> There was a great deal of pressure. People were running scared. You can't have much luck trying to implement behavioral change in a survival environment. It's much easier in a young, dynamic, and growing organization. If you don't get a critical mass going, it's not going to last.

So, the program evaporated.

There are a number of lessons to be learned from the Spacetronics experience. First of all, it is clear that significant increases in production and in quality can be achieved from a program such as the one which we have described. It is practically impossible to single out

exactly the impact of each of the different components of the program—training, goal setting and feedback, communications and joint
problem solving, or the redesign of jobs and the flow of work—but
the common element seems to be the implementation of a participative approach between supervision and the work group. Where objectives are jointly developed and shared and problems jointly solved,
high levels of commitment and resulting high levels of performance
tend to follow.

The Spacetronics experience also demonstrates the need for a catalyst to keep the program moving. The psychologists in the Human
Factors Group and Harry Baker, the outside consultant, played a
very important role in initiating the strategy and guiding first-line supervision in how to move toward a more participative supervisory
style. For this to happen, too, there clearly had to be top-level support. The active involvement of George Carson, factory manager,
and Jim Garber, overall head of manufacturing, was essential.

But it takes more than just these components to sustain a program
for changing a total management system such as that attempted at
Spacetronics. There has to be some stability in the system—stability
in terms of work load, in terms of people, and in terms of technology. At Spacetronics, the downturn and reduction in force by
roughly two-thirds was just too traumatic for a program such as this
to sustain itself.

Perhaps if the program had gone on for a longer time and it had
been possible to achieve a real "critical mass" of supervisors and employees experienced in and committed to operating under the new
system, it might have lasted. Perhaps! But so far we have no evidence
more than a hope that this can, in fact, happen. But with the potential payoff that is clearly there, it certainly should be worthwhile
for more organizations to test whether or not a participative system
can, in fact, be sustained if a critical mass is achieved.

7

A Participatively Designed Pay Plan*

Absenteeism—chronic and excessive—is one of the most insidious drains on productivity of any of the forms of employee withdrawal. When an employee fails to show up for work, the job does not get done, or quality slips as teammates attempt to cover for their missing co-workers, or schedules are disrupted as personnel are shifted to fill the void. In many technology-keyed operations such as assembly lines, start-ups may have to be delayed with down time and frustration for undermanned crews and significant productivity losses.

Absenteeism is no small problem in the United States. Figures prepared by the Bureau of Labor Statistics in 1974 state that 4.3 million nonfarm wage and salary employees—out of a total of 74.9 million workers in that year—were on unscheduled absence each week. Of these, 1.8 million workers were absent for the entire week and 2.5 million for part of the week, averaging two days. Absenteeism in the nonfarm sector of the economy in 1974 added up to approximately 39.9 million hours per week from short-term absences and an additional 70.9 million hours per week lost from full-time absence. The rate has been relatively constant over the last few years and significantly did not decline in the face of escalating unemployment in 1974. The productivity implications are obvious.

Such absenteeism tends to concentrate in lower level jobs. The experience of a small, Connecticut-based manufacturing and cleaning service organization—The Sanitary Group—was typical. The Sanitary Group has three lines to its business: a manufacturing organization

*Lawler, E. E., III and Hackman, J. R., Impact of employee participation in the development of pay incentive plans. *J. Appl. Psychol.* 53 (6): 467–471 (1969).

Scheflen, K. C., Lawler, E. E., III, and Hackman, J. R., Long-term impact of employee participation in the development of pay incentive plans: A field experiment revisited. *J. Appl. Psychol.* 55 (3): 182–186 (1971).

preparing cleaning materials and specialty chemicals and paper supplies, an industrial laundry service, and a building maintenance and cleaning contracting service.

In the late 1960s, somewhat over one hundred people were employed by The Sanitary Group. The business was growing rapidly, to the point where there were almost 400 employees in 1976. In the contract cleaning side of the business, which included the largest number of people, most of the workers tended to have very low educational levels, and most were members of minority groups. Approximately half were female, and most of the men undertook the job as a second job or moonlighting. The ages of the employees ranged from sixteen to over seventy. The employees were not represented by a union.

Mickey Nunes, one of the two partners running the firm and the partner with responsibility for the contract cleaning services, recalls that in the late 1960s, "whatever we were doing, it was obvious that it wasn't right." Turnover in the work crews was extremely high, absenteeism was a chronic and pressing problem, productivity tended to be low, and the commitment of the employees in general was very bad. The situation, in his view, required some radical new approaches:

> We were very traditional managers. We tended to be relatively authoritarian. My own background and training was in the military, and my approach was one which believed that if somebody is told to do something, they do it. Thus we all had some difficulty in understanding how the new generation questions authority and doesn't exhibit commitment to participate in the organization.

About that time, Nunes became oriented to many of the concepts which were emerging from the behavioral sciences. He developed a close personal relationship with a well known and dynamic spokesman for applied behavioral science concepts and began to gain some insight into the importance of behavior on the part of management in enhancing work force productivity.

As a result, Nunes started a number of actions designed to turn the organization around. He initiated a series of steps designed to change the leadership climate of the organization and build a more participative Theory Y orientation. The main thrust of this approach consisted of sending most of the key managers to laboratory sensitivity training sessions, as well as holding workshops and sessions internally.

This type of training was concentrated solely at the upper level of the organization. To combat the relatively low level of commitment reflected in high absenteeism and turnover among the crews in the contract cleaning part of the business, Nunes engaged two researchers from a nearby university to work with the organization in designing programs.

As they focused on the problems and the nature of the employee group and the requirements of the jobs, the researchers decided to concentrate on designing a pay plan specifically tailored to the prevention of absenteeism. Recognizing that the employees generally were part-time workers, often had short-term dollar objectives which they were trying to satisfy, were generally unskilled, had relatively limited career interests, and felt relatively low organizational or job commitment, the researchers felt that a simple and direct incentive plan was probably the best approach to get employees to respond positively in efforts to reduce absenteeism.

At the same time, the organization was an ideal setting for testing some additional concepts which behavioral science theories suggested would be important in enhancing employee commitment. Specifically, the researchers decided to assess whether or not the process of obtaining full employee participation in the design of a pay incentive plan would have an impact on the extent to which the plan operated effectively. They were able to do this because workers in the contract cleaning side of the business were broken up into a number of crews servicing different client accounts but all doing essentially similar work. By having some of the crews design their own pay plan in a very participative fashion and by implementing the plans in a more imposed fashion in other groups and then comparing the results, the researchers would be able to determine the extent to which participation could be a positive factor in gaining response to an incentive plan to reduce absenteeism.

The researchers picked nine groups—without visiting or talking with them but purely on *a priori* grounds—to be included in the study. Although the groups were not exactly comparable in terms of types of cleaning assignments, an effort was made to have them as nearly equal as possible. The groups were similar in terms of the average age, the worker's education, experience, social class, and so forth.

Three of the groups, of ten, nine, and eight members, were assigned to be in the "participative" condition. That is, in these groups the workers would have the major voice in deciding how the pay plan would be structured. Two other groups with thirteen and twenty-six members would have the pay plans imposed upon them without a voice in their design. Finally, two other groups with nine and eight employees served as control groups. While the researchers did plan to talk with these groups, there was no change in their incentive scheme. Their performance was tracked for comparison purposes.

The researchers met several times with each of the participative teams to help them evolve their own pay plan. At the first meeting, a member of top management introduced the researchers, explained why they were there and that the company was concerned about absenteeism, and emphasized that the researchers' role was to help in developing an appropriate plan for rewarding good attendance. The top manager then left the group, and the researchers worked directly with the team. First-line supervisors were present at the meeting but were told not to enter into the discussion.

Not much was accomplished during the first meetings, which tended to be relatively long (about forty-five minutes). The workers expressed a great deal of skepticism, mistrust of management, and mistrust of the researchers. They tended not to believe that they really had the opportunity to design their own incentive plan but demanded to know what kind of a plan management really wanted. The researchers responded to this by reemphasizing that their role was merely to serve as resource persons and that the employees did, in fact, have the opportunity to design a plan for themselves. After about forty-five minutes, the researchers suggested that the employees talk some more among themselves about a plan and suggested that they should reconvene the next night.

At the second meeting, there was still considerable mistrust, hostility, and skepticism, but more progress was made. The group began to focus on the actual process of designing a plan, and the researchers served as resource persons but did not give any direction or guidance to the specific nature of the plan. The focus in all three groups was on determining a bonus to be paid for full attendance.

One of the groups began to evolve a plan that had a very high bonus, on the rationale that "since the company will cut whatever we ask for in half, anyway; the bonus should be large." The other groups, however, were much more conservative. One of the researchers recalls:

Someone in the group would say, "No, that's too high," and they would pull it down themselves. Management's secret fear was that they would ask for the moon and management would have to say no, you can't have the moon, and they would say, "see, it's a fraud anyway." That didn't happen. They were, in our view, very responsible about what an appropriate amount was.

Four meetings were required for two of the groups to come up with a final plan and three meetings for the third. All of the plans were agreed to by all of the group members. There were some differences in the plans as they were evolved. Two of the groups wanted their bonus computed on a weekly basis, and the third group used a monthly basis. The number of days of sick leave that would be allowed and the size of the bonuses requested also differed to some extent.

The plans were presented to management by the researchers and they were quickly accepted with minor alterations. The amount of the bonus was made equivalent for all three groups, and what would constitute excused absence from work was clarified. All three of the plans paid $2.50 a week for perfect attendance by these part-time employees. The bonus was paid on a monthly basis to one of the groups and on a weekly basis to the other two. These changes were explained to the members of each of the groups, and the plans were implemented.

For the two "imposed" groups, with thirteen and twenty-six members, identical plans were set up. For one of the groups, payment was based upon a weekly computation and for the other group payment was based upon a monthly computation. There was only one meeting with each of these groups and at the meeting the reason for the plans and how they operated was explained fully.

The researchers visited with two of the control groups, which had nine and eight employees, and discussed problems of absenteeism, turnover, and incentives. However, no incentive plan was installed in these groups. Two other groups served as control groups with twenty-six and eight employees. Attendance data from these groups were monitored, but the researchers did not talk with these employees.

For the twelve weeks prior to the implementation of the incentive plan, attendance in the three "participative" groups averaged 88 percent. During the sixteen-week period immediately after the plan was implemented, attendance averaged 94 percent. Thus, the average rate of attendance improved by 6 percent, which was a significant improvement.

In the two "imposed" groups, attendance was 83 percent in the twelve weeks before the plans were implemented, and remained at 83 percent during the sixteen-week period after implementation. There were also no changes in the rate of attendance in the four control groups. Thus, the results clearly suggested that an attendance incentive plan, *if* implemented with full employee participation, could significantly increase the rate of attendance over a sixteen-week period. Merely imposing a plan such as this, however, had no impact over the short-term period.

The researchers recall that initially there was a great deal of skepticism about the plans in all groups. But gradually, as the employees saw that management meant what it said about paying for performance and as they started to get their bonus dollars, the plan began to work in the participative groups. Employees in the imposed groups continued to exhibit considerable skepticism, even after sixteen weeks.

In the face of this demonstrated success in the three participative groups, it is extremely interesting that two of the groups discontinued the plan within twelve months, one of them after six months, and one of them after eleven months. Only one of the three groups continued with the plan beyond a year.

In the two groups where the plans were discontinued, attendance had been running at the rate of 92 percent for the nine-week period before they were discontinued. However, for the five-week period after the plan was discontinued, attendance dropped precipitously to 82 percent. It seems clear that discontinuing the plan resulted in a significant decrease in attendance. In the one group where the plan remained, however, attendance held up at 93 percent for a twelve-week period starting a year after the plan had been implemented. Also, in the two groups where the plan was imposed, follow-up a year later showed that attendance had increased to 87 percent (from 83 percent before and immediately after the plan was implemented). Presumably, after a year members in those groups realized that the incentive was not a trick, and it gradually took hold and began to work.

The results clearly suggest that the incentive plan did function effectively to increase employee attendance. This is particularly true in the participative groups where the results of the plan were felt rather rapidly (within sixteen weeks after implementation). It took longer for the plan to be felt in the imposed groups, but gradually it did pick up effectiveness and attendance did increase.

Why, then, was the plan discontinued in one of the groups after six months and in the other after eleven months? Herein lies one of the more useful insights from this case study; certainly more useful than the results suggesting that an incentive plan can, in fact, impact attendance behavior.

A number of factors seemed to be at work. The researchers placed heavy stress on the fact that they failed to obtain the involvement and commitment of the middle levels of the organization. The researchers were originally brought in by Mickey Nunes, a senior manager who was highly committed to the program. The researchers worked directly with the work teams and middle management was told not to get involved in the incentive plan at all. The noninvolvement of the middle managers in the incentive plan was a fatal mistake according to the researchers. They reported how, shortly after the plans were implemented, many middle managers expressed skepticism and dissatisfaction with the arrangements. Some managers began to call the incentive plan the "bribe program," since they felt the plan was bribing employees to come to work. In their view, such a plan was just plain "wrong." There were even some indications that there may have been an attempt to actually "sabotage the plans" on the part of middle management.

Senior management, which was highly committed to building a more participative and open climate in the organization, became increasingly dissatisfied with the resistance of upper middle managers in the organization. In the view of Mickey Nunes, "the Peter Principle was taking hold with some of the people at higher levels." He became increasingly impatient at their persistence. As a result, a systematic program to replace the managers at the middle levels and bring in new people was initiated. In hiring new managers, Nunes set criteria for individuals who were more open, participative, and more interpersonally skilled than the former management team.

As the new managers took over, productivity went up significantly. However, at the same time, the incentive programs began to be eliminated.

Nunes indicates that he would like to see his managers retain the plans and move into a more open and participative style; but he points out the double bind that he is in.

> You can't go in by fiat and tell them to maintain the incentive plans. Then you're not a Theory Y manager. If I say "do it," they can point a finger at me, and they're quick to, and say, "what the hell's participative about that? If you want to be autocratic, go ahead and be autocratic. Tell us what to do and we'll do it.

But as Nunes observes, "unsaid, but clearly implied, is 'and then you've got the responsibility if it doesn't go well. Don't call us back.'" So, having given his new group of middle and senior managers the authority and the responsibility to get the job done and with them delivering results in terms of significant productivity increases, the plans could be discontinued purely at their own discretion, and Nunes could do nothing about it if he truly wanted to follow his own participative philosophies.

The new middle managers' decisions to discontinue the programs were not all as irrational as it might seem on the surface. One of the characteristics of the work force in this particular organization was high turnover. The average tenure was ten months. As a result, the crews began to be staffed by individuals who had not been involved in the original design of the incentive programs. With middle managers being less than fully committed to the programs since they were not involved in their design and implementation, there was little attention to indoctrinating new employees into the rationale and operation of the plan.

Very quickly, the incentive rewards were taken for granted and seen as part of the basic pay. More and more, behavior began to slip back and absenteeism increased. Workers wanted to get the reward even when their attendance did not warrant it, and they made excuses as to why they should get it anyway.

One senior manager relates a story about a senior female employee with ten to fifteen years of service. On one occasion, the foreman deducted the bonus, as the plan called for, and the employee "went through the roof." She went to higher management and got the bonus reinstated.

As managers found it increasingly difficult to get the incentive reward concept across to new workers, they began to see the plan as more of a nuisance than as a help. Their response was to discontinue the plans. It was quite evident that in the press of day-to-day business, they lost sight of the fact that the first research data had indicated very positive results.

In summary, there are a number of reasons why the plans tended to be eliminated:

1. Management below Mickey Nunes was resistant because they had not been involved in the initial design of the programs and they philosophically were not committed.
2. The researchers who had been responsible for keeping the programs alive were no longer on site.
3. When new managers came in, they did not understand the program and did not have a sense of ownership. They were achieving positive results of increased productivity and felt less need for the incentive plan.
4. With high turnover in the work crews, employees felt no sense of ownership and began to take the bonus as a right.

Gradually the plans were eliminated, and, within five years, none were in existence among the part-time cleaning crews.

Mickey Nunes would like to get the plans reinstated. But, with his new management team and his concern about maintaining a participative climate, he cannot force the issue. Part of the problem is the fact that the organization is small and there are limited resources. He would like to bring the consultants back in but his managers feel that the money should be spent elsewhere—"why should we be paying for high-powered consultants when we need that new equipment?"

The results of this case suggest that successful implementation of change requires participation and ownership of the program at each level of the organization impacted by the change. Also, continuing education of the employees involved in the plan and orientation programs for new personnel are needed to insure that the principles of the program are maintained and understood.

With regard to a participatively designed program in a situation of relatively high work force change, there needs to be an opportunity for "reparticipation" every so often. As one of the managers in the Sanitary Group points out,

> I'm not sure of the validity of an employee-designed pay plan designed by a group of ten people in which, five years later, none of the ten are still in the group, but the same bonus plan is still in effect. Now, do the new people have a right to redesign it or not? They've inherited the plan but were not part of the original design. That's the same impact as having the plan imposed.

He has a very valid point. There needs to be some monitoring of the degree to which the work force feels ownership of the plans and, when this ownership feeling is low, there should be some form of intervention.

At this point, the Sanitary Group will probably not go back to a bonus plan for attendance. While Mickey Nunes would like to move in that direction, he feels powerless to do so. The rest of the management team feel they are getting the results they need without the bonus plan. They recognize the need for some continuing support and educational effort, if they were to put in a bonus, but do not feel it is warranted in an organization of their size.

There are a number of lessons to be learned from this case study. First of all, it does appear that employee participation in the design of a pay incentive plan can be an important ingredient for obtaining support for and acceptance of the plan. Contrary to many expectations, employees were found to be very reasonable in their design of an incentive plan which was acceptable both to management and employees. Organizations should be aware of the potential mileage they can achieve from getting the employees involved in the design of equitable reward systems.

The case also illustrates the importance of gaining management commitment and support throughout the participative design process. Participation does not mean going around the heads of middle management. To do so will surely alienate them, and their lack of support will lead to the demise of the program.

Also, there does appear to be a need for "reparticipation" from time to time, especially in an environment with high turnover. People need to feel a continuing sense of ownership and responsibility for programs which are set up. An ongoing system of communications and problem-solving groups, such as those discussed in the next two cases, may be a useful approach for achieving this sense of ownership and responsibility.

At the very least, this case demonstrates the potential positive benefits that can be obtained through employee participation in the design of programs and policies which directly effect them. Participative management, in practice, can be an important strategy for enhancing productivity and quality of working life.

8
Turning Around a History of Labor/Management Conflict

The automobile industry has been the scene of some of the most intense confrontation and conflict in the history of labor/management relations in the United States. The confrontations of the 1930s were the culmination of a long struggle by unions for recognition by the company and for the representation of all workers in the industry. These confrontations in the 1930s set the tone for the next thirty years of labor relations in the automobile industry. The dialogue between labor and management was rigidly polarized into a we/they orientation—an approach to relationships fought in terms of win or lose situations. Union demands were always for more: whatever the traffic would bear. And all dialogue about demands for more were saved until formal contract negotiations. On the management side, the way to get ahead was to be as tough as possible with the union: do not let them get away with anything; show them who is boss; operate on the philosophy, "When in doubt, throw them out."

In the 1950s and 1960s, the XYZ plant of the AHM Corporation served as a prototype of the rigidly polarized orientation of labor/management relationships. There was a great deal of strife and conflict and the plant was seen throughout the AHM system as a hotbed of industrial relations problems. There were constant confrontations between union and management which resulted in grievances and walkouts. As John, the personnel manager put it, "it was a constant state of war." John, who came to XYZ in 1967, stated that he "inherited a declining environment. In 1968 and 1969 everything was going the wrong way in terms of absenteeism, costs, walkouts, and so forth." The plant was at the bottom of the AHM system in quality, production, and efficiency.

In 1968, a merger brought about increased concern over how to get better cooperation in the plant to improve efficiency and productivity. The problem of improving efficiency and productivity was compounded by an atmosphere of extremely hostile labor/management relations. Then, in 1970, perhaps partly because of the efficiency problems in the plant, the production of trucks was moved to another facility. Truck production had always been looked upon as a mainstay of the operation. Its loss, in the view of Angelo, Superintendent in the Body Department, "really shook people up." Rumors and fears began to spread that the plant would close because of its low efficiency and escalating costs. Almost everyone began to recognize that something had to be done—and soon—in terms of improving efficiencies and productivity in the plant. But there was no clear consensus about how to break away from the pattern of vicious labor/management conflict, worker apathy, and substandard production performance.

In the early 1970s the AHM Corporation was promoting a process of Organization Development (OD) to improve relationships and performance in its various operations. Several members of management went to an AHM sponsored seminar on OD and became quite enthusiastic about it. In the face of the obvious need for improvement, the OD process was quickly embraced as a way for potentially turning the situation around.

Bob, of the Training Department, recalls how the plant began to push OD with a great deal of enthusiasm. Seminars were held, communications sessions were conducted, and supervision was encouraged to provide feedback to employees. But, Bob recalls:

> The behavior in the plant was just not ready to accept OD. Supervisors were judged by how tough they were. But, after going through the OD process, people began to expect their supervisors to make them happy. Then, when it didn't work immediately, everybody reverted back to the old style and the word went around that OD doesn't work.

Ralph, Chairman of the Union Shop Committee, pointed out that the union found much of the emphasis promoted in the OD effort to be offensive. The reaction was particularly negative to a corporate film.

It was as if AHM wanted to have the fruits off the tree before they were willing to plant the tree. We'd been telling them for twenty-five years that if you treat me as a human being, you'll get the fruits, but they weren't ready to really do it yet.

Many people feared that the plant was one step away from a shut-down. It was clearly recognized that something had to be done to turn the situation around. But, with the apparent failure of the OD effort there was still no clear idea of just what should be done. Then, almost by chance, dramatic changes began to occur. The process started in the Hard Trim Department where the exterior trim on the automobile—the taillights, the moldings, etc.—is installed.

As part of the production reorganization following the abandonment of truck production, a group was meeting to review plans for new production facilities. Representatives of industrial engineering, the plant engineer, the superintendent, staff planners, and so forth were working together to design the most efficient layout for the new production model. It was almost by chance that something unheard of happened in the meeting of this planning group. As Bob relates it:

Someone raised his hand and said "Hey, here we are. We don't do any work. But here we are trying to figure out the best way that it should be done. Maybe we should ask the people that actually are going to do it. They probably know a lot about it that we ought to use too." So they decided to involve the people in the design. It had never been done before. You just don't do those kinds of things.

Thus, the planning group began to ask the people on the line what they thought the layout for the new production model should be.

So, a year in advance of the production change, each employee in Hard Trim was given an opportunity to comment on the layout and what would be most useful to him or her in the way of tooling and facilities. The focus was also on how to build the facility so that it would accommodate two shifts.

The idea grew during the year, and a similar approach was undertaken in the Soft Trim Department (upholstery, seats, etc.). People started presenting their ideas and most of them were glad to contribute. Some of the workers, Bob recalls, would say: "Don't bother me. Do what you gotta do, pal, just let me do my job." But the majority of the employees did make contributions. The design of the new production layout involved a year of working with all of the employees to be affected by the production change. Bob describes the results:

D-day finally came. After all this planning, each Supervisor checked that his/her employees had the proper stock, materials, and knew what they were supposed to do. Then the button was pushed and the line got rolling. They got the jobs through the trim shop, all the way around; downstairs to soft trim, all the way around, and over to the chassis department—just like it was a normal everyday day. It was a perfect start-up. Unbelievable! The best that it had ever been done in the history of the plant, ever—bar none. People were amazed.

This experience started a whole chain reaction. It was not an OD effort; it was building a grass roots understanding that perhaps employees do, in fact, have something to contribute in the decision of how to most effectively organize and run the operation. The success of this experience led a number of departments to involve their employees in planning changes and problem solving.

Not all of these efforts to involve employees were as successful as the dramatic start-up in the Hard Trim and Soft Trim Departments; there were still some problems. But, in general, when the new approach of involving employees was implemented, the problems of employee relationships were not the monumental ones that everyone had grown accustomed to and had expected.

For example, at one point the Body Shop had been experiencing 35 percent bad welds. Management decided to involve the employees in trying to get to the bottom of the problem and helping to solve it. So they approached the employees as follows:

Hey guys, we don't know what the problems are. We need your help to try to find out why we're having these problems.

And they scheduled a series of problem-solving "rap sessions" to try to jointly evolve the solutions.

A number of things came out of these sessions, including the need for training, better materials, different tooling, maintenance, concern about absenteeism, and so forth. Within several months, according to Bob, the average weld discrepancy was reduced to 1.5 percent from 35 percent—a 95 percent reduction—as a direct result of the involvement, cooperation, and problem-solving efforts of the employees.

A similar approach was used in the Metal Finish Department. Improper metal finishing was causing problems in the Paint Shop. The employees from the Metal Finish Department worked directly with Paint Shop employees to try to solve the problem and come up with different finishing approaches. The result of these joint efforts was a dramatic decline in the number of metal finish problems and improved performance in the Paint Shop.

Another example of the success achieved through the involvement of employees in problem solving occurred with the process of putting the simulated wooden side decals on station wagons. Formerly, this decal placement had been done in an off the line operation which was very disruptive to the assembly line. In searching for a way to apply these side panels more effectively, management gave the problem to the employees to solve. As a group, the employees came up with a new way of applying the decals so that the process could be done directly on the line without the disruption and loss of productivity. Under the former philosophy, management would have tried to dictate a solution or change, and it probably would have failed.

Bob points out how the new approach represented an entirely different philosophy from OD.

> Under OD, the approach was one of "here's my problem, what can you do about it." Under this system, though, the approach is "here's our problem, what can we do about it." We're not trying to make people happy. What we're trying to do is involve them, utilize their talents. We started to believe that people had some smarts and that they want some control over their own jobs.

Gradually the union began to take a more active role in the problem-solving dialogues. The experience in the Body Shop became typical throughout the company. All along, as management began to involve the employees in problem solving, the union had been kept fully informed. The department began holding regular "rap sessions" of ten to twenty people to deal with various problems and gradually, the employees became more and more involved.

In 1974, a joint union–management committee was established to oversee the enhancement of quality of working life in the plant. To some extent this committee was the result of the initiative and encouragement from the AHM Corporation. But the fact of growing receptivity and understanding about the value of cooperative problem solving locally at XYZ made the establishment of this committee more feasible.

At this point, an outside consultant was engaged to deal with union and management representatives to help make the process of enhancing the quality of working life more effective. The consultant was necessary, not only because of his expertise in areas of worker participation, but also because an impartial party was needed to help union and management learn to work together in a cooperative venture rather than a negotiating one. It was the first time that such a project was undertaken with the union and management sharing equally in the planning and decision-making responsibility.

There was, of course, mistrust of management for the union and vice versa which stemmed from their years of conflict with each other. However, mutual agreement was soon reached on the objectives of the participation program. According to Bob:

> If people just tell you about their problems, you get nowhere. But when you start involving people, meaningfully, in tasks which affect their jobs, they start to derive some satisfaction from that. They have something to say about the achievement of their goals, their ideas, and the way they work. We all bought into that. What we're in for, together, is satisfaction. The way we get satisfaction is by dealing with the tasks people do. The goal is satisfaction—it's not productivity. But we know we'll get productivity too.

Productivity is a disturbing concept to most unions because traditionally, when managers think of productivity, they think of efficiency and of cutting people. However, there are many other ways to achieve productivity, and these were the areas which the union–management committee began to push: waste, quality, planning, housekeeping, scrap, absenteeism, and so forth.

The committee's approach was to ask for volunteers who wanted to participate, to provide them with training in problem-solving techniques, and to create teams which would focus on getting the job done more effectively and on things that were making the job difficult or uncomfortable. The teams would develop alternative ways of doing many jobs. Management would then decide whether it could accept the alternatives based on the information that was provided to them. Although the union was initially wary of this approach, when they saw that it was a genuine effort to improve the quality of work life as well as effectiveness, they gradually "bought in."

An experience in the Soft Trim Department shows how this approach turned into a win/win situation for everybody. In Soft Trim, two out of the sixteen supervisors in eight areas volunteered to try the team approach to problem solving. This particular area had had a history of very bad problems in quality and in employee relationships. An area meeting was held and out of the sixty employees who attended the meeting, thirty-four decided to try the joint problem-solving approach. Training was held after hours and additional meetings were conducted to consider severe problems of glass breakage, molding damage, and water leaks, among other things. These meetings were held after work with the teams' members being compensated for one-half of the meeting time.

The teams worked on the aforementioned problems and for about one month there were some good results. However, at the beginning of the second month attendance began to drop off because of rumors of a massive layoff. Two weeks later, nearly 2,000 employees were laid off and the team problem-solving experiment was postponed.

After the layoff only twelve of the original thirty-four member team remained. They were anxious to resume the experiment, so four months later these twelve members, along with a new supervisor, continued where they had originally left off.

Glass breakage was a severe problem in the area. In addition to disrupting assembly, each broken windshield cost between thirty and forty dollars. Eighty-six windshields had been broken over the forty-three-day period prior to the team's focus on the problem of glass breakage. The team worked out a number of changes to help reduce breakage, including such straightforward things as padding the I-beams nearby with foam rubber. The result of these changes was a dramatic reduction in the amount of breakage. For the twenty-one-day period after the changes were made the level was down to only seventeen broken windshields. At the breakage rate experienced before the joint labor/management problem-solving effort, forty-three windshields would have been broken over the same twenty-one days. In the ensuing months, the rate of breakage remained low.

In tackling the problem of excessive water leaks around the windshields, the employees tested management's true commitment to the cooperative problem-solving approach. In the Soft Trim Department the operation of sealing the windshields and back windows traditionally had been done by two persons. However, the process had been changed so that one person did the total process. Following this change, the number of cars per day with windshield water leaks increased from around 200 to over 360. The employee problem-solving team took on the task of trying to determine ways to reduce the excessive number of faulty installations.

In the problem-solving session the employees brought out a number of problems with the new operation such as: unsafe conditions, more water leaks, and poorer product quality. In trying to solve these problems the employees attempted to find a solution that would benefit both the employees and the company; they were successful in their attempt.

The suggestion to return the second person to the operation as well as some other changes recommended by the team were adopted. Very promptly, the number of water leaks dropped dramatically to about fifty leaks per day. As a result of this experience, the union recognized that there could be something in the direct problem-solving approach both for management *and* for the union. As Ralph, Chairman of the Shop Committee, summed it up:

> As it worked out, we gained a man, and the corporation saved money.

Gradually, the spirit of a more cooperative and rational approach to problem solving began to enter into the more formal aspects of labor–management relations. Bob highlights the change:

> In the negotiation process, usually everybody waits with long lists of demands. Then they come into the negotiations and they sit around and bang on the table. Then you take that list and go back and say, "yes, we can give them that; no, we can't give them that"; it's a long process.

But now, our union began to come in with things that made sense. And we told the union, "great, don't wait 'til contract time. If it's a good idea, let's take care of it right away."

As trust began to grow between union and management based upon experience and the more enlightened approach to negotiations, the spirit of cooperation began to spread into other areas impacting the operation of the plant. One of these areas was the area of work-related discipline.

Management began to focus more and more on ways to change the behavior of supervisors with regard to work-related discipline. Bob outlines the change in philosophy:

We may have 5 percent that are considered problem people, but 95 percent of them are good. We've set up all our rules to control the 5 percent, and the other 95 percent have to live by those rules. Unfortunately, when we manage for the problem people, then everybody lives like the problem people. So we turn everyone off and turn everyone sour.

We began to ask, why do we do that? Why do we perceive all people as problem people? We should be doing things for the 95 percent of the people that are good employees, not the 5 percent. Give the people the benefit of the doubt.

So the staff and superintendent group developed a basic philosophy about work-related discipline and how to approach it. The emphasis was on helping to solve the person's problem, rather than taking disciplinary action.

The approach to work-related discipline was through a joint commitment on the part of the shop committee and supervisors to talk with people who seemed to be having work-related problems. The main idea was to solve the problem constructively before it escalated into a major issue. To facilitate this communication, a number of small offices were installed on the shop floor which could be used for talking over problems and attempting to solve them. The union, management, or an employee could initiate discussion to get at the heart of the problem before it reached the state of a formal grievance or disciplinary action.

As problems were solved more and more on the shop floor, the grievance load dropped dramatically. At one point in 1975, there were only two grievances in the system (in a plant with 2,000 employees) and both of these grievances were wage related; in effect, there was nothing the plant could do about them. These two grievances compare with the load of well over 500 grievances in a similar period in 1971. Both management and labor directly attribute this decrease in the grievance load to the new spirit of joint labor–management cooperation and problem solving to handle problems on the floor before they get locked into the formal grievance procedure. Ralph puts it:

The committee people were able to get out on the floor and handle the everyday problems before they got out of hand and had to be processed as written grievances.

Angelo, the Superintendent in the Body Department, points out the difference:

Grievances can wrap you up. Years ago, we had 5,000 or so, and some plants still have this thing going. The thing is that when you sit down with a committeeman, or even before a grievance is written, that committeeman gives you the consideration to talk it over. The simplest thing is to take a piece of paper and write a grievance. But that doesn't get the damned thing solved. It will be in the mill for another three or four months. Instead, we get out on the floor and talk to the people, "What's your problem?" before we take to discipline. But the point is, sit down with the committeeman and work the problems out, and the answer may be, "no, you don't have it coming, you're not getting it and here's the reasons." A good 90 percent of the time, it can be worked out, if you have good relations and good reasons. And, vice versa, if there's a justified request, they get it. Like a fan or ventilation problem, or time off, or vacations, and so forth.

Once in a while, the quality of working life idea has been misused. For example, when someone is suspended for good cause, an employee may say:

Hey, you can't do that, it's not quality of working life.

But today the union and management committee will sit down and work it out together, clarifying what is and what is not a fair way to proceed.

The new system of labor–management cooperation and problem solving has shown up in results in other areas besides grievances. Absenteeism reached a peak in the conflict-filled years of 1968 and 1969. Since that time, the absence rate has declined sharply and has remained at or below the "bogey" which was set for absenteeism at 5 percent.

On various production indices, it is difficult to track exact trends at XYZ because of changes in the models being produced and due to the fact that a shift was lost and then added back in the last few years. However, the significant point is that the plant has gone from being near the bottom in the AHM system on many production and quality indices to being one of the best in the system. Quality ratings improved dramatically during the period of the middle 1970s; XYZ is now at or near the top in warranties, scrap, and efficiency.

Angelo says, "We're No. 1," and attributes this fact almost 100 percent to the problem-solving approach which they have undertaken. He outlines the different spirit that is responsible for the change:

> Years ago a guy would send garbage down the line and never even think about calling you, because years ago we'd never listen. Now, a guy calls you, you listen to him, because what he's doing is trying to tell you he has a problem. It might be a bad run of material and something doesn't look right to him, even if it's not in his operation, and he's not responsible for it. But he's involved, and he wants someone to listen, and we will listen.

So, the consensus of all parties involved—management, the employees, and the union—is that the environment is vastly different in the latter 1970s from what it was just a few years earlier.

What was responsible for these seemingly dramatic and/or basic changes in what had been an entrenched system of conflict and low productivity? As in most changes in real systems, it is impossible to pinpoint any one factor that is responsible. A number of forces were at work.

First of all, the plant was in trouble. Operating costs were escalating out of sight. The climate of entrenched labor–management conflict caused the plant to be seen as a problem location throughout the AHM network. Management was considering closing the plant. Then, with the reorganization, the loss of truck assembly production, and the reduction to one shift in the economic downturn of the early 1970s, everybody—management, the union, and employees—realized that their own job future depended upon improving the situation.

At the time the changes were most needed, XYZ was fortunate in having a plant manager who was well liked by all of the people in the plant. He was solidly behind the idea of labor–management committees working to enhance the quality of working life in the plant. He supported the work of the committees and gradually the heads of management in the plant came around to a more receptive attitude toward new ways of thinking. The climate which he set, in the view of both the union and of management, was very important in initiating a new direction for relationships.

Another important factor which contributed to change was the success of a "grass roots experiment" which involved the employees in the design of a new production system. To the amazement of many in the plant, the process worked! The success of this process in the Soft Trim and Hard Trim departments, probably as much as anything, helped to open the eyes of both management and union to some new ways of approaching problem solving. The fact that there was a clear need for change and a favorable climate for change facilitated this, but the demonstration of the fact that employee involvement can lead to dramatic positive results probably was the major catalyst for more widespread change.

The people saw the role of the consultant as helpful in bringing about change. In the various training programs which the consultant ran and the problem-solving sessions at which he assisted, his role was one of keeping the efforts on cooperation between the union and management in getting the problem solved. His role was an important one, though not the primary one behind bringing about change.

Similarly, there was a supportive atmosphere from the AHM Corporation which was helpful, though not the key factor behind the changes. The corporate OD program, as we have seen, was actually kind of a "false start" for the plant along the road to change. However, support from AHM for the concept of labor–management joint committees to enhance the quality of working life did give the concept official sanction and support; further support at the plant management level reinforced that and helped to make it happen.

Such things as a list of "operating principles" for employee relations which the AHM Corporation has distributed to management also helped to provide a climate for the types of changes which took place. These six principles are:

1. Discuss with the union representatives and communicate with employees information that affects them as far in advance as possible.
2. Establish effective means whereby union representatives can communicate with management outside the scope of the grievance procedure.
3. Treat with respect and consideration employees and their representatives as a fundamental ingredient of the resolution of mutual problems.
4. Abide by the spirit and the intent of all signed agreements and verbal commitments.
5. Encourage the prompt resolution of complaints prior to their being reduced to writing.
6. Resort to formal discipline only after other reasonable corrective measures have failed.

These formal "operating principles" reflect the official position of AHM toward employee relations practices and are useful in setting a tone which can be translated into reality.

In addition to an emphasis on quality of working life on the part of the AHM Corporation, the International Union has been working to set a climate for improving labor–management relationships. There have been some dramatic experiments in new forms of organization and relationships in which the union has been participating with several managements, including AHM. In the union's relations with AHM, a climate of more openness, mutual respect, and joint problem solving has begun to evolve at the corporate level, and a new form of dialogue between senior management and union representatives has also begun to take place.

This clearly can set a tone for the local union. But at XYZ, the union representatives feel the impact has been minimal.

Our aim is not to please the International. Our aim is to please the workers at XYZ. It's a local program, and we're moving ahead on our own. Each plant will have to do it their own way and when necessary seek the aid of the International.

Angelo sums up his feelings about the change process:

You have to change because times are changing. I was a believer in the old whip deal, you know. But it wasn't paying off. It wasn't doing right by me or the organization. So you accept that. You have to make a change. If you don't make a change, they're going to change you. You just can't treat these people as children. They're adults, and they want to be treated as adults.

So, in the 1970s, there has been a dramatic change in the climate and in the operating results at the XYZ plant of the AHM Corporation.

The big question, of course, is "Will it last?" The people think that there is a very good chance that it will. The changes have survived several shifts of management and seem to be picking up momentum and spreading more widely through the plant. The changes seem to gain more credibility each day as they demonstrate that they are effective in improving the working conditions for the employee as well as the production and efficiency return for the company.

Ralph says:

The only way the program will fail here is because of management. We were very skeptical, and still are not thoroughly convinced. But 90 percent of the people would say that it's a hell of a lot better here than it was six years ago. The only way the program will fail here is because of management.

And on the part of management, Angelo says:

We're committed. The total management group is committed. I'm an old line manager, but I see where we're going. I see this is a necessary part of building the automobile. Because I've been there where we had the old system, I can see this is easier for the people. I think it's easier for the supervisor too. So we're committed.

It just may be that the XYZ plant of the AHM Corporation can serve as a prototype for changing the kinds of entrenched labor-management conflict and discord which has been so characteristic of much of American industry over the last fifty years. If so, it is one of the more significant practical experiences in enhancing the quality of working life and productivity and deserves careful study and emulation.

9
Transplanting An Open System of Management From One Organization to Another

One of the most dramatic and attention-getting experiments in new ways of organizing the people aspect of a company took place in the early 1970s at a plant of General Foods Corporation in Topeka, Kansas. This plant, which manufactures Gaines dog food products, was designed to incorporate many of the concepts which had emerged from the applied behavioral sciences over the last twenty years. The objective was to build a plant which would maximize utilization of the human resource and be a model in terms of good quality of working life.

Most of the innovations incorporated into the design of the Topeka plant have been widely publicized. They include such things as:

- Careful attention to the selection of new employees and a full orientation prior to hiring about the new method under which the plant would operate.

- Personnel in the plant had a direct voice in the hiring decisions.

- Personnel were organized into autonomous work teams which had direct responsibility for deciding many of the production and organizational issues involved with getting the work done.

- Responsibility for getting the work done was carried by the team and the interchange of jobs and functions at the discretion of the team members was a necessary ingredient.

- Daily self-measurement techniques were developed so employees were continuously aware of performance in costs, production, and waste.

- Pay levels were based upon merit and the level of skills which the team members had attained.

- A climate of very open sharing of information, participation, and communications was built at all levels in the plant.

The results achieved by this experiment were dramatic in terms of productivity and favorable attitudes on the part of employees. The project received worldwide attention and was viewed by many as a harbinger of the future in terms of organization in American industry.

Bob Mech was Manager of Manufacturing and Services at the Topeka plant of General Foods. As such, he was deeply involved in the design and implementation of the experimental program. As part of his involvement he met many of the visitors from various companies and other organizations who came to the Topeka operation to observe and learn about this new form of organization. One of the people he met in this capacity was C. Angus Wurtele, Chairman of Valspar Corporation, a 170-year-old Midwest paint company.

Valspar is a firm with $60 million sales per year and about 1,000 employees in six paint and three plastic plants. For a number of years, Angus Wurtele had been looking for a way to improve the productivity and quality of working life in Valspar. Although part of his motivation was to find a way to make a low capital base organization compete effectively with larger organizations, he was also sincerely interested in new ways of organizing which would increase the quality of working life for employees. He visited the Topeka plant in the middle 1970s as part of his search for new organizational systems which might be useful within the Valspar organization.

It is no coincidence that in March 1975, Bob Mech left the Topeka plant and became Plant Manager at the Valspar paint manufacturing plant in East Moline, Illinois. The primary customers of the East Moline plant are the large farm implement manufacturers located in Moline—John Deere and International Harvester. The Valspar plant employs about forty-five persons with twenty-seven in the hourly work force. In 1974 the plant produced 1,384,000 gallons of paint.

The production and employee relations climate at the East Moline facility was less than fully satisfactory. When Bob Mech was brought in as Plant Manager the following conditions existed: turnover was running at the rate of 187 percent; there was an 11 to 12 percent absenteeism rate; there were product quality problems with 50,000 to 60,000 gallons of unusable paint sitting out in the backyard. In addition, customer returns of defective products were running at a high rate—100,000 gallons in 1974.

As an additional indication of the climate in the plant, just two years before Mech arrived, the plant had been organized by the Painters and Allied Tradesmen. The reasons for the organization, according to Mech, were strictly internal—not due to any one specific thing, but a general disenchantment on the part of the employees with how they were being treated had caused them to organize themselves. Clearly, the situation was unsatisfactory, and one of the main reasons that Mech was brought in was to change the system by using many of the concepts which had been developed at Topeka.

Mech, a firm advocate of the open system form of organization which had been implemented at Topeka, firmly believed that a similar approach could help to solve many of the problems at Valspar in East Moline. However, he did not want to move too fast as he felt very strongly that employees had to "buy in" and participate in this open system form of organization voluntarily. He went relatively slowly at first and spent a great deal of time working with his staff in orienting them toward the open system of organization.

Mech also held orientation sessions with all of the employees in the plant. As he recalls:

> I spent a great deal of time explaining that this is why I'm here. I explained to them "in reality, anything that's done will have to be done as a group. I'm not going to dictate. If nobody wants to change, that's fine. I see my role as making those changes and supporting that kind of activity that you really want to do. But it's going to be up to you."

According to Mech:

> Building trust takes a long time. It's a little frustrating. But I'm very satisfied today, at least as far as I'm concerned. I still have some problems about management in general, but as far as I'm concerned myself, I think people really buy in that I'm going to be fair. I'm not going to squabble over things that don't mean anything. So we have very few, if any, problems over meaningless things. There's only been one grievance since I've been here.

Thus, a large measure of the approach toward building a more open system in East Moline revolved around generating an atmosphere of trust and openness; the personal style as a manager which Bob Mech brought to his assignment was probably the major single catalyst for setting the proper climate for change.

Mech's approach was to try to make the people in the plant aware of some of the factors which tend to detract from a good quality of working life and some of the different ways of organizing which might help to enhance it. He used the "traditional model" presentation which had been developed at Topeka. The model outlined the key factors detracting from quality of working life in traditional organizations and served as a jumping-off place for discussing areas where changes might be brought about. An outline of the model is shown in Fig. 9-1.

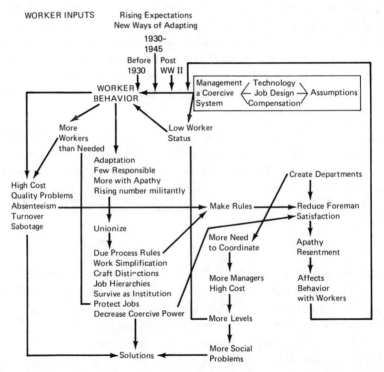

Fig. 9-1. The traditional model. (Reproduced with permission of L. Ketchum, Westport, CT.)

Mech recalls that after he had been at East Moline for about two or three months he spent one whole Saturday going over this model with the total population from the plant. He pointed out to them:

> This is what I believe. If people start taking a look at this model, we can start to change some of these things which make organizations less effective.

He recalls:

> The younger guys got into it quickly. The more senior guys had more trouble, though, and were less willing to buy in that traditional forms of organizations so frequently led to negative consequences.

A number of changes in ways of operation were made at the East Moline facility as part of Mech's continuing effort to build up trust on the part of employees. First of all, several guarantees were made to employees: Nobody would be hurt as a result of any changes made; if the plant "turned on" and became profitable, some form of sharing of the gains with employees would be instituted. In explaining these guarantees, Mech pointed out that the present level of productivity in the plant was not adequate and that the corporation was not getting a fair return on its investment because people were not really participating and producing. Thus, there needed to be some improvement on the part of the employees to get the return up to the point where it was fair to the corporation. Then, he said, if there were further returns beyond that, he would work to institute a gain-sharing program with the employees.

Some of the other things that were done shortly after Bob Mech came to East Moline were:

- Employees were given the responsibility for scheduling their own batches in manufacturing paints. The mixers had responsibility for deciding in what order the batches would be produced and the mill operators scheduled their own work.

- Break buzzers were eliminated and employees were able to take their breaks at their own discretion.

- Employees were involved in the interviewing and hiring process and made recommendations about specific job candidates as they came through.

- Reserved parking spaces were eliminated.

- Job rotation was permitted on an informal basis. This was not put through as a formal program as previous experience with an imposed system of rotation had been poorly received. But informal rotation, on employee initiative, of the relatively monotonous jobs of mixing, leading down, and filling on the second shift was encouraged.

- Employees were encouraged to accompany marketing personnel in reviewing customer complaints.

- A safety committee was organized and was headed by a plant employee.

Bob Mech's efforts to open up the system and build trust obviously have had some success. The union steward for the Painters and Allied Tradesmen—Bill Christensen—expresses his reactions:

You know, he took his name off the door and got rid of the reserved parking place. You can sit at the table right here and I can sit in his chair if I want to, and it wouldn't make any difference. And, I don't know, I think some of the people look at it—hell, he's just the same as I am. And nobody has any problem coming in here to talk with him. Any of the guys can, I don't have to for them. If anyone has any problems, they can come in and get it straightened away.

Bob Mech points out that not all of the changes that he would like to see implemented "take." For example, employees still punch the time clock. He has made it known that it is not required to punch. But, he says, "I'll be damned if I'll go out and tear that clock out of there. They have to do it." So they continue to punch, out of habit.

Another example of a change that did not "take" pertained to working hours. Mech was willing to set up flexible hours for employees in the office but the people were doubtful of this practice and expressed concern that some of the "others" would take advantage of it. So flexible hours never got off the ground.

However, Mech points out that change takes time, and he is optimistic that things are moving in the right direction.

We started involving people more in things they had never been involved in before. In terms of costs, we tried to review with everybody at a plant meeting every two to three months what's going on and let people know how things are; what things are important to the business. Then we get them together by groups to work out changes. And that's when they started changing the scheduling in how people work. I tried to stay out of a lot of those changes but only provide the stage for doing it. I was very cautious not to have the changes be my program. It's frustrating, at times, but I'm willing to take the time to let people really buy in.

Mech comments on some of the changes which the employees have made:

Take employee visits to customers. Where we've used it, the problems just go away. For example, one of our customers was complaining to the salesman about having the stencil identifying the contents of the drums on the top of the drum. It would stand out in the weather and then they couldn't read it after awhile. The complaint went up to the sales organization, then back down through manufacturing, and by the time it got to our people on the floor, nothing happened. So the salesman took some of our people out to the customer where they could see first-hand what the problem was, and the problem went away. The same kind of thing happened with complaints about dirty paint, and so forth.

The process of enlarging the point of view of production workers has been instituted extensively at Moline.

A lot of our people had never seen the end use of our products. So, every Monday for three to four months we took them through one of the local tractor plants in groups of four or five. The salesman went along. It was a tremendous asset in building their concern about the quality of our products.

Al Anderson, first-shift production foreman, pointed out that people liked being involved and having a say in the hiring process and that this employee involvement helped to build a different climate in the plant.

If you do have a problem with someone, they can't say "Boy, that Al can't pick people." It puts the responsibility on everybody. It's *we* made a mistake, not *you* made a mistake.

Bill Christensen, the union steward, points out that:

The atmosphere is, oh, a lot different than it was before. It used to be, if I go and take two smoke breaks in the morning, I'd hear about it. Now, I wanna take three smoke breaks, nobody says anything. I think the other guys feel the same way—if they want a sandwich, go have a sandwich. No problem. A cup of coffee, or whatever you want. There's nobody standing over you saying: "hey, you can't do this. You had one too many smoke breaks this morning, or something." It used to be that way. You had to go hide to have a smoke somewhere. Now people don't have to hide. It stops the bullshit, as long as you don't overdo it. Then you get somebody else saying, "Hey, you going to stand around all day bullshitting?" Nobody's gonna let you take advantage of a good thing.

The proof of the pudding is in the results, and it looks as if the results at Valspar in East Moline are very positive. The most dramatic results in terms of productivity are in the area of product quality. Bill, the union steward, provides some understanding of why this may have happened.

You're most aware of test batches now. It seems like a challenge. "Hey, it's a new customer and we've got to make them happy and get a good product out." We can't slop around here and slop around there. I think everybody takes pride in what they put out, for this reason—that's quality, and this customer could amount to a $100,000 a year contract or something like that, you know. The information—we get it. The guys are pretty well informed. And they react this way. I know I do. If I get a challenge, I love it. If there's a new customer, or somebody comes down from Minneapolis and I work with him, hey, I enjoy it.

Such concern about product quality is being expressed in tangible results. While returns from customers were running about 100,000 gallons a year in 1974, in 1976 they were reduced to 4,000 gallons. And where the plant was "sitting on" fifty to sixty thousand gallons of bad product when Bob Mech came, this has now been reduced to seven to eight thousand gallons.

Al Anderson points out that the more open climate makes it possible to correct errors in blending of paint before they get out of hand, whereas before a whole batch might be lost.

The climate in the plant is much more open now. People are more apt to talk about things. If you make a mistake, they'll tell you, whereas before they probably wouldn't say anything. There's better working conditions all the way through. People care more about the work that they do.

Results have been positive in other areas besides just quality. Turnover has been reduced from losses of thirty-six people in 1974 in the hourly group to only two people in 1976. Absenteeism has been cut almost in half, and only one lost-time injury was registered in 1976, while there were four lost-time injuries in 1974. Table 9-1 highlights some of these trends.

Bob Mech feels that these positive results are "90 percent from new organizational system." But, there is some frustration because he is not sure how to use the increases to sustain this kind of program. Volumes have been relatively flat: 1,384,000 gallons in 1974, 1,160,000 in 1975, 1,280,000 in 1976, and no real growth in 1977. The plant is capable of producing 1.5 to 1.6 million gallons. But, being tied to the farm equipment industry, the potential for increasing volumes is just not there. So, Mech finds it hard to know how to follow through on his desire for gain sharing with employees from increased productivity when the need for productivity increases is not there.

Table 9-1. Three Years of Operating Data
Valspar Corporation—East Moline, Illinois

	1974	1975	1976
Turnover (percent)	187	22	9
Absenteeism (percent)	Not Available	11.2	5.7
Doctor Cases	19	20	18
Lost-Time Accidents	4	3	1
Disabilities	2	0	0
Unshippable Product (gallons)	50–60,000	16,796	7,800
Bad Product (destroyed) (gallons)	Not Available	2,643	179
Product Returns (from customers)	100,000	12,168	4,191

We need the volume and growth. In this situation, people are going to get terribly frustrated. If we had the volumes, we could really make this place hum. There might be a lesson here about innovation. You talk about productivity and if you don't need it, why mess around with it. It's kind of frustrating.

Not all of the experiences at East Moline have been positive. In December 1976, the plant went out on strike for a week. The employees wanted personal days added into the union contract based on an incentive for attendance—something which had been negotiated by the UAW with the farm equipment manufacturers in Moline. However, Bob Mech refused to put an incentive for attendance into the Valspar contract as it was "against my grain." His feeling was that the jobs should be sufficiently rewarding for people to want to come to work without an external incentive.

Employees went out on strike on Wednesday. Mech recalls:

On the Tuesday before the strike we shipped more product between 7 A.M. and 12 P.M. than we normally ship in two weeks. We had 12 semi's out back which we filled. I told the employees, "We've got customers to satisfy and we need to get the product out. You guys have to have a job to come back to." It was tremendous. Every guy showed up for work. It was a lousy night, but they were running around out back looking for product to ship. The union steward worked right along with us. I wish I could explain it. There was a tremendous reaction the day before they went out on strike.

Mech attributes this reaction to the high level of commitment which had been built up under the new system.

Bob Mech feels that the organization is moving into a new level of maturity after several years of experience with the open system.

The organization is just beginning to accept the fact that those things that don't get done are not necessarily my fault. I'll accept the majority of the blame for it, but I'm not going to accept the blame for those changes that we don't get done. If I have to call the shots on everything, then we haven't changed anything. And if you—whoever you are—are really interested in doing something, then you damned well ought to be sure that it gets done. And I'll support that, but don't blame me if it doesn't happen.

The East Moline facility of Valspar Corporation seems to have made a definite turn toward an open and self-governing system. The results are evident in terms of product quality, employee commitment, and low levels of absenteeism and turnover.

The changes at Valspar clearly have resulted, in large measure, from the personal style of Bob Mech. He is highly dedicated to the open system of organization which he helped to develop at the Topeka plant of General Foods. His personal style and enthusiasm in building a more open system in East Moline was infectious in the organization and gradually, as he puts it, the system was "bought into" by all but the most skeptical. The system seems to be working.

The transformation of a total system such as seems to be taking place at Valspar probably takes the degree of dedication and commitment that Bob Mech was willing to give. This type of transformation cannot be done overnight. And it certainly needs a vision—a model of what might be done in an organization—to make it happen. Mech brought both the dedication and the vision to East Moline. He was also blessed with a charter from Angus Wurtele to make the open system of organization happen. So far he has been able to make the system work but he is facing the critical task of sustaining the momentum which is obviously underway in a no-growth environment in which he is frustrated from sharing the gains of productivity with employees. Whether gains sharing is an essential component for the long-term vitality of open organizational systems such as Mech has been evolving at Valspar remains to be seen. The next few years may provide the answer.

Interim Summary for Chapters 6–9
Illustrating Humanistic Change Efforts

The dynamics of the changes taking place in these four cases are much more difficult to pin down than was true of the cases we included under the rough designation of "behavioral" innovations. What was done in these four organizations, to a considerable extent, smacks of the whole "marshmallow" of the behavioral sciences. The changes were not like the relatively neatly contained concepts of goal setting, schedules of reinforcement, or performance feedback included in the previous cases.

In addition, the more dramatic of these cases are not nice, clear, controlled experimental studies. The experiments being done at the AHM Corporation and at Valspar are not matched with control groups against which comparisons may be made. Yet the results still appear dramatic. The qualitative evaluation—the excitement and the enthusiasm evident within these organizations—clearly suggest that significant and pervasive changes are taking place.

Although the changes in these four organizations are not as crisply identifiable as the behavioral innovations, there do appear to be several common components. First of all there is the theme of increasing employee participation in significant decision making in all four of these organizations. Participation was the explicit factor studied in the design of a pay system at the Sanitary Group, and employee participation seemed to be the key factor resulting in the significant reduction in absenteeism. At Spacetronics, increased employee participation in problem solving, in determining working conditions, and in setting performance objectives was the common thread throughout most of the projects which were undertaken. And certainly at the XYZ plant of the AHM Corporation, the employee/

management problem-solving groups entailed a large element of participative management. At Valspar, the work group was taken as the total plant because it was small enough, and the total thrust of the changes at Valspar has been to get employees to take more responsibility for deciding on the work conditions and how the plant should be run.

Another common theme through most of these cases is the building of a climate of openness and trust. The original skepticism of the employees in the Sanitary Group about the sincerity of management in letting them design a pay plan had to be overcome. At Spacetronics, there was a great deal of work with the supervisors to shape their behavior so that they placed more trust in employees. And clearly at the AHM Corporation and at Valspar, the direct thrust of the effort has been to develop a climate of mutual trust between management and employees.

Finally, a common theme of all four of these cases is a high level of senior management support. Such support is essential as an umbrella under which new forms of organization can flourish; without this support not much of substance will take place.

The innovations in two of these organizations appear to be healthy on a relatively long-term basis; in two, the organizations have reverted back to practices of earlier times. In the Sanitary Group, a key reason for this reversion was the lack of middle management support for the innovations. Because middle managers had not been involved in the design process they did not really "buy in" to the participatively designed pay plans. Then, on the slightest excuse, the plans were discontinued.

Changing times proved to be the downfall of the program at Spacetronics. With a work force reduction of roughly two-thirds, the participative program just could not withstand the resulting upheaval of the organization.

An open issue in these broad-scale total systems changes is the question of gains sharing with employees. The only case in which this was explicitly part of the change was in the Sanitary Group where employees received a direct incentive for attendance. However, with lack of continued emphasis by management and no orientation of new employees to the nature of the program, the incentives quickly became taken for granted. At that point they were no longer seen as a sharing of gains but as a given right. From then on, the program fell apart.

Gains sharing was not built into either the Spacetronics or the Valspar experience. Whether the gains achieved at Valspar can be sustained without sharing them with employees remains to be seen. At the AHM Corporation there has been implicit gains sharing as the plant has become profitable and a perceived possibility of shutdown has been circumvented. The gains are seen as significantly improved working conditions and increased job security, for all concerned. Whether this will be adequate in the long run again remains to be seen.

These four cases, as a group, reflect the potential productivity and quality of work life gains which can be achieved by taking a more enlightened viewpoint of the American work force than has been traditional in many organizations. By recognizing that employees are concerned about their own conditions of work, that they do have the potential for bringing to bear insights and innovations for better ways of doing the job, and by organizing in such a way that they have this opportunity, significant improvements can be registered. What is needed is a supportive senior management and climate, a commitment on the part of local management to bring about change, and a willingness to take some risks. It has been done in these four organizations—plus many others—and it can be done in others. The productivity payoff can be substantial.

Flexible Working Hours to Enhance Productivity and Employee Morale*

The concept of flexible working hours is one of the newer areas of human resource management with which many organizations have been experimenting. Flexible working hours entail changes in organizational policy and practice regarding conditions of work which can have a direct effect on employees' personal autonomy and discretion.

The practice of flexible working hours originated in Europe during the 1960s and very quickly obtained widespread acceptance. Since then, such programs have increasingly been adopted by firms in the United States. By the mid 1970s, the concept of flexible working hours probably had become the most significant and extensive structural change that a number of organizations had adopted in order to increase the employee's control over various aspects of the working environment.

Some traditional managers have looked upon flexible working hours, or "flexitime," as a chink in the armor of management prerogatives. On the other hand, organizational theorists who are concerned with modifying traditional bureaucratic and authoritarian management systems to fit in with the changing requirements of a postindustrial society have viewed flexitime as a relatively painless first step in the process. Organizations which have tried flexitime in the United States have experienced, as have many European firms, an almost universal increase in employee morale, or, at the very least, no decrement in morale. The implications for employee pro-

*Golembiewski, R. T., Hilles, R. and Kagno, M. S., A longitudinal study of flexi-time effects: Some consequences of an OD structural intervention. *J. Appl. Behav. Sci.* **10**(4): 503–532 (1974).

ductivity from these early experiments are less clear, though flexitime at least does not appear to have a negative productivity impact.

The case study we are about to describe shows how an organization with a relatively cautious, if not negative, posture with regard to introducing flexible working hours changed its attitude to a position in which flexitime was actively endorsed and implemented throughout a wide range of functions.

The concept of flexible working hours is a relatively simple one. Basically, it is a process which allows employees a certain amount of discretion with regard to their starting and stopping times each day, with the requirement that the total number of hours worked within a designated period meet some prescribed standard. For example, one model of flexible working hours gives employees discretion in terms of the time at which they start work each day. There is the requirement that all employees have to be at work during a core period in the middle of the day, for example, between 9 A.M. and 3 P.M. Around that core period, however, individual employees may have the option of starting work any time between seven and nine o'clock. The requirement might be, then, that they work eight hours plus one-half hour for lunch, leaving work eight and one-half hours after the time at which they started. For example, if they started at seven o'clock, they would be permitted to leave at 3:30 P.M.; if they started at nine o'clock, they would be required to work until 5:30 P.M. This would be an example of flexible working hours within the workday.

A more advanced model entails flexibility within the workweek. Here, employees are required to work a certain core period within each day, but they may start and stop work each day at whatever times outside of the core period that are most convenient for them. The only requirement is that the total workweek add up to some specified number of work hours.

Figure 10-1 illustrates this type of system. Here, all employees are required to work the five-hour period between 9:15 A.M. and three o'clock. However, on any given day they may start as early as seven o'clock and leave work as late as six o'clock. Thus, potentially, they could work a ten and one-quarter hour workday (allowing forty-five minutes for lunch). Then, if the requirement is to fulfill a thirty-five-hour week, employees would balance out the total number of hours

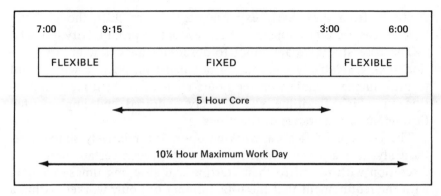

Fig. 10-1. Flexibility within the workweek—"flexitime."

worked to fulfill that minimum requirement. Of course, they would have to work each of the five days of the week for the five-hour core period.

Some problems may be encountered with this plan because of the wage–hour laws of the Walsh–Healy Act which specify that non-exempt employees must be paid overtime for all hours over eight hours worked in a day. However, if the scheduled working hours are less than forty in a week, there is some discretion allowed; if the scheduled hours equal forty, then each day must consist of eight hours or else overtime will have to be paid. In effect, then, for non-exempt employees on a forty-hour week, flexibility within the work-week is not possible, although flexibility within the workday, as out-lined above, is.

A further extension of the concept of flexibility within the workweek might drastically reduce or even remove the core work hours imposed on each workday. If the core work hour requirement were removed, in the example shown in Fig. 10-1, employees conceivably could complete their thirty-five-hour work requirements in three and one-half days of the week, leaving one and one-half days for time off. This schedule could be arranged entirely through their own discretion to meet their own personal requirements.

Some flexitime programs go even further than this, allowing employees to "bank" time from one week to the next. Thus, it might be possible to work for several weeks on a ten-hour per day schedule and then take a block of time off corresponding to the hours saved up in the "bank." These programs, of course, have to work within the requirements of the wage–hour laws which require overtime to be paid to nonexempt employees for workdays of more than eight hours or workweeks longer than forty hours. With exempt employees, however, these laws do not apply, and such liberal and imaginative flexitime programs are permissible.

There are a number of potential advantages from instituting a flexitime program. For one, overtime may be reduced. When employees find themselves in a work situation which should be finished on the spot for maximum efficiency rather than deferred to the next day, they may do so without incurring overtime costs. In the same vein, productivity may be enhanced because they are not required to discontinue work in progress in order to avoid overtime but may complete it and thus avoid the productivity loss entailed in a second start-up the next day. Also, employees are able to balance for themselves when they will work on projects to a greater degree than under traditional working hour arrangements. Thus, employees who feel they are most productive in the early hours can arrange their working schedule to maximize this fact; similarly, persons who feel they are most productive late in the day can adjust their schedules to accommodate this fact.

In addition to the above advantages, a flexible work hour system can also accommodate the employee's need to go shopping or to attend to other personal business. Flexible work hours should thus eliminate the employee's need for special permission for absence—or unexcused absences—to attend to personal business.

Potentially, there should also be a reduction in sick leave. Employees who oversleep should not feel it necessary to call in sick because they can adjust their schedules to make up the lost time.

Finally, one would expect that a flexible working hours program, which permits employees more discretion with regard to their working hours, should have a positive impact on morale by increasing the employees' feelings of control over the work environment, by providing a means for overcoming annoyances such as commuting traffic jams, and perhaps by increasing the level of awareness and concern on the part of supervision in balancing out work requirements and in understanding the activities of individual employees.

However, in spite of all these potential benefits, many supervisors are skeptical of the flexitime concept. First of all, many managers are concerned that communications will be impaired when the only certain time that all employees are present is during the core hours. In addition, for some jobs which are tied very closely to technology—such as assembly line work—it may not be possible to leave positions unmanned at the discretion of the employees. Also, it is frequently necessary to use time clocks to account for working hours, and many managers anticipate that this practice will have a negative impact on employee attitudes. In addition, there is often the concern that it will take an excessive amount of supervisory attention and time to manage a program such as this. Whereas traditional methods have built-in control systems which do the job effectively, flexitime requires managers to be aware of employee attendance and to be sure that work loads are balanced and that there are sufficient employees present to keep the work moving. In the final analysis, probably the biggest objection to flexitime is based upon the fear that supervisors will lose control when the decisions with regard to working hours are delegated to employees.

All of the preceding objections were raised at SmithKline Corporation, in Philadelphia, when a proposal was put forward in 1972 to institute flexible working hours. SmithKline Corporation is engaged in the manufacturing and marketing of health care products. It is a multinational corporation with headquarters in Philadelphia and has a total of 14,000 employees. Roughly 3,000 employees work in the Philadelphia area in a variety of administrative, research and development, manufacturing, and marketing positions.

In 1971 the Personnel Department had put together a proposal to implement staggered work hours in the Philadelphia-based operations of the corporation. The proposal resulted from some familiarity with staggered work hours programs in the United States. The concept of flexible work hours fitted in with the organization's philosophical commitment to try to increase employee self-determination and participation in decision making in the corporation.

However, the response was negative when the proposal to implement staggered work hours was presented to the Corporate Operating Committee. Senior management rejected the proposal for all of the reasons outlined above as potential problems with flexible work hours.

In the Spring of 1972, however, one component of the Research and Development Division, at a suburban location called Upper Merion, independently approached the Personnel Department to explore the possibility of establishing summer working hours. For a number of years the possibility of establishing summer hours had been raised, but a change had never been implemented. Basically, the Upper Merion unit of the Research and Development Division wanted to start earlier (at 7:45 A.M. instead of at 8:45 A.M.) during the summer months in order to increase the number of daylight hours at the end of the day. The change was suggested based upon the general feeling that there was a strong desire by Upper Merion employees for this arrangement.

In response to this suggestion, Rick Hilles, who was then the personnel representative to Research and Development, put together a proposal which emphasized a change in the existing work hours rather than a temporary change of hours during the summer months. This change in work hours was proposed as a means of enhancing productivity and improving morale.

The proposal which Rick Hilles presented to Research and Development management was to test out a pure flexitime within the workweek program. The specific program he proposed was the one outlined in Fig. 10-1.

After considerable discussion, Research and Development management agreed to support the proposal. Employees at Upper Merion felt that if a change were to be made it should be a significant departure from the old system of fixed working hours. At the same time, however, management agreed that the program should be undertaken as a test to obtain some experience and data about the actual impact of flexitime.

At this point Rick Hilles was in a bit of a bind. He had gained the interest and commitment of Research and Development managers up through the top level Vice-President but at the same time he did not have the corporate blessing to institute flexible working hours; in fact, the Corporate Operating Committee had been specifically negative to the prior recommendation for work hours experiments.

At this point the Vice-Presidents of Research and Development and Personnel provided crucial support for the proposal and prevailed upon the company President to permit a pilot test of flexitime. Although the President continued to have strong reservations about the program, he agreed to the test in order to get better data on its impact. Several circumstances were favorable to the decision to go ahead: the implementation of fleximite was to be tested in only a limited part of the organization, it was implemented only as a test, and the senior manager was actively supportive of the test within his area of functional responsibility.

Within the Research and Development organization at Upper Merion there were three significant units which totaled fifty-eight people. Over half of these employees were professionals who held B.S., M.S., and Ph.D. degrees in chemistry and biology. Other members of the groups consisted of technicians, clerical, and secretarial personnel. Two of these groups, consisting of thirty-seven people, were interested in trying the fleximite experiment. The manager of the third group was negative to the proposal. His main objection was the use of time clocks to record arrival and departure times. This situation provided a natural experimental design for testing fleximite. It was decided that the program would be implemented in two departments and the third department would be used as a control.

The experimental design involved the measurement of impact at several points:

1. Data were collected prior to any changes in all three of the departments. The data consisted of a questionnaire survey of Upper Merion employees' and supervisors' opinions about working hour practices and their impact on various operations, as well as objective data dealing with hours worked, absenteeism, supporting costs, etc.
2. Comparable data were then collected six months after the implementation of flexible working hours.
3. Final evaluation data on the same types of measures were collected after twelve months of experience with the program.

The results on the "objective" data on overtime, absenteeism, and costs were favorable but not completely conclusive. There was a significant decrease in overtime during the first six months of experience with flexible working hours, and it remained at a low level during the final six months. The reduction in overtime was by approximately 75 percent. However, it is not possible to attribute this reduction directly to the flexible working hours program. During the period of the experiment there was concerted management emphasis on reducing overtime; there were changes in work assignments and missions which obviated the need for much overtime; and many of the employees in the experimental units were not eligible for overtime so the potential for change was relatively limited. On balance, however, SmithKline feels that, at the very least, the flexible working hours program did not have a negative impact on the efforts of management to reduce overtime.

With regard to absenteeism, there was a reduction of 35 percent in total paid absenteeism in the two experimental groups compared with a 15 percent increase in absenteeism in the control group. However, these results, as well, are not completely conclusive, as the rate of absenteeism in the experimental group had been running at a relatively high rate initially in comparison with the control group. At the same time, however, there was a slight increase (15 percent) in single-day absenteeism in the experimental groups. This contrasted with a 21 percent increase in the control group. However, for a number of reasons, it is not possible to state conclusively that the experimental groups exhibited a significantly better absenteeism record than the control groups. At the very least, however, the flexi-time program did not have a negative impact, and it probably had a positive impact on absenteeism.

A review of the distribution of starting and stopping times during the period of the test (Table 10-1) shows that there was actually a relatively small spread in the times in which most employees came to work or left work. The median starting time, during the test period for the winter months was 8:45 A.M.—the same starting time that was required under the original work hours program. Almost two-thirds of the employees started or stopped work within fifteen minutes on either side of that median time. During the summer months from April to August, the median starting time moved forward by fifteen minutes to 8:30 in the morning. Again, the majority of employees came to work in a relatively small interval of time around that median. Thus, the actual impact of flexible working hours, in terms of employee presence or absence during the traditional period of working hours, was relatively slight.

There is an interesting point brought out by the data in Table 10-1

Table 10-1. Work Hour Patterns

TIME	WINTER MONTHS (NOVEMBER–MARCH) PERCENT OCCURRENCES	SUMMER MONTHS (APRIL–AUGUST) PERCENT OCCURRENCES
ARRIVAL		
7:00	0.3	0.8
7:15	1.7	2.6
7:30	6.5	7.3
7:45	3.2	5.1
8:00	4.5	7.5
8:15	12.0	15.0
8:30	20.9	23.1
8:45	25.3	18.2
9:00	16.6	11.8
9:15	6.9	6.7
9:30	1.9	1.7
DEPARTURE		
3:00	1.3	2.8
3:15	7.2	11.1
3:30	5.5	6.7
3:45	3.9	4.7
4:00	5.1	6.1
4:15	6.4	7.7
4:30	15.1	14.1
4:45	20.8	17.7
5:00	12.7	9.8
5:15	8.1	6.8
5:30	5.1	4.8
5:45	3.7	3.0
6:00	2.3	3.2
6:15	1.1	0.9

which reflects these work hour patterns. During the summer months, only 16 percent of the employees elected to come to work at 7:45 or earlier; almost 40 percent started at the traditional starting time of 8:45, or even later. This suggests that had Research and Development implemented a summer hours program as they had originally intended, starting work at 7:45, it would have appealed to only a distinct minority of the employees. Such a program probably would have had a negative morale effect if management had implemented it "in its infinite wisdom" about what employees preferred. The flexible working hours program, on the other hand, allowed employees to exercise their individual preferences for the working schedule that they wanted.

The attitude survey results, which compared opinions about working hours before the program, after six months of experience, and after twelve months, provide the most impressive demonstration of the impact of flexible working hours. Figure 10-2 illustrates a composite overall reaction of participants in the pilot test to some eighteen questions dealing with working hours. These questions cover:

- degree of participation in decisions about work assignments;

- degree of difficulty in scheduling work requiring others;

- satisfaction with current work hours;

- reaction to use of time clocks;

- traffic congestion encountered to and from work;

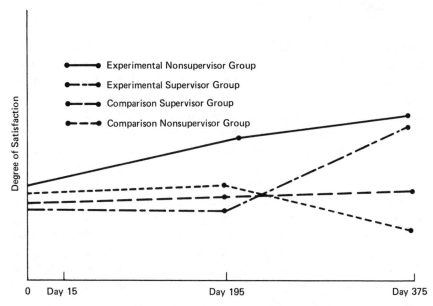

Fig. 10-2. Flexitime pilot test summary results.

- ability to handle personal business during the workday;
- impact of current work hour policy on individual productivity;
- conflict with co-workers over scheduling work;
- individual's flexibility to schedule work assignments;
- desirability of respondent's department as a place to work;
- quality of communication about work assignments;
- conflict with supervisor about scheduling work;
- availability of others when help is needed;
- ability to arrange meetings with others when necessary;
- inclination to work more than the standard workweek;
- quality of communication about company activities of personal interest;
- availability of others for "spur of the moment" discussion or phone calls;
- quality of support services.

Figure 10-2 illustrates clearly that there was a significant increase in favorability of response by employees to these questions during the first six months of the flexitime program and that these favorable attitudes held up between the six- and twelve-month checkpoints. For supervisors in the experimental groups, however, there were no particular changes during the first six months, but in the second six months favorability of attitudes increased significantly. The degree of favorability to these eighteen questions for employees in the control group was relatively stable across the total twelve-month period.

Figure 10-2 suggests that employees very quickly became positively disposed toward these working hour issues after the implementation of flexible working hours. Even more significantly, their positive attitudes were sustained throughout the full twelve-month period. The twelve-month duration of these positive attitudes contrasts with more costly changes in hygiene items, such as pay and benefits, which have been shown to have a short-lived positive impact.

Supervisors, on the other hand, appeared to have more of a "wait and see" attitude. Their attitudes did not change for the first six months but, after a certain amount of experience with the program, they did become significantly more favorable to the point where their opinions at twelve months matched those of the employees. The fact that the attitudes of employees in the control group did not change suggests that the positive improvements in attitudes were a result of the flexitime experiment rather than some extraneous influence in this Research and Development environment.

The write-in comments by employees on the questionnaire illustrate very dramatically how the employees felt about the program. Write-in comments on the survey taken at twelve-months were universally favorable. A few examples were:

I'm very much in favor of flexible work hours and feel that they make it easier to schedule work assignments. Since many experiments cannot be readily adapted to a rigid set of working hours, the flexible hour concept has been a real asset to research and development work.

Extremely positive. It is often more efficient to complete certain operations in one longer day. There is more incentive to do this by starting earlier and working a little later if the time can be "carried over" until later in the week. Better morale—if one is having a really good day there is incentive to keep going longer. If it's the kind of day when everything is going wrong, it's okay to leave early!

The flexible work hours are a boon to the working person. They give the worker an opportunity to be his own boss in the small segment of his job. At present, these hours are the only thing which makes my otherwise unbearable job bearable.

The flexible hours policy has helped my job attitude—even though my job is always routine, some days it can seem more so and on those days instead of looking at the clock constantly, I can just leave and make up the time on my energy days.

Flexitime has been a good innovation. I would like to see it continued. It has caused no real difficulties with scheduling of work.

People are available when needed. There are always people who take advantage of the situation, but for the most part, people have been acting as responsible adults.

The time clock—which at first seemed objectionable—now is seen as an aid in timekeeping and proof of time worked. As long as everyone is on the clock it's okay.

I feel there is a new sense of operational unity and a smooth interaction in working. There is no drop in efficiency. There is a positive approach to complete assignments with the feeling you are working for the company and, in turn, this work schedule aiding you. I also think that fixed times, fixed habits had put people into a deadening rut and it seemed to disappear. I see this positive effect very much in myself.

I see flexitime as a no-cost (to the company) fringe benefit that seems to be paying off well in terms of improved morale. This, in turn, leads to more positive attitudes toward the company and inevitably greater productivity. PLEASE KEEP IT GOING IF AT ALL POSSIBLE!

The write-in comments by supervisors on the twelve-month survey were also uniformly positive. For example:

The current flexible work hours are an excellent system. I can make much better use of my time both at work and away from work. I find myself planning the work I'm going to do for the day more regularly now than I did with the standard working hours. Also, it is a tremendous boost for morale. Just great!!!

It is the best system I've worked under to date. It inspires a very positive attitude toward the company and willingness to go out of one's way to "repay the favor."

Current work hour policy is excellent. It allows more freedom to schedule routine assignments on a day-to-day basis. It is easier to arrange personal matters outside of normal working hours. It boosts morale and productivity, since people feel they have somewhat more control over their lives.

Significantly, in the survey, on questions dealing with employee productivity, both employees and supervisors felt that the flexible working hours arrangement was having a very positive impact. Although it was not possible to measure productivity directly in this Research and Development environment, it seems safe to conclude that the program did have a very positive effect on employee attitudes and probably on productivity as well. At the very least, there was no productivity cost associated with the flexible work hours program.

Following this test in the Research and Development organization, Rick Hilles presented the results to the Corporate Operating Committee. The write-in comments on the survey and the other data provided a convincing picture of the positive benefits which could be obtained under flexible working hours. After considerable deliberation, and with endorsement from a task force which was studying methods for enhancing the quality of work life within the corporation, a most remarkable change in corporate policy took place. The President issued a directive that he wanted each major functional unit of the corporation to examine the flexitime approach and then develop a form of flexible work hours that was suitable to their operating needs and responsive to the preferences of employees. He went a step further, moreover, and informed managers that they would have to justify their decision to him if they decided not to implement a flexible working hours program. From being an active skeptic, if not opponent, of flexible working hours, he became a positive endorser, if not promoter, of the concept. At the same time, the President also decided to implement an exception reporting system which did not require the use of time clocks in implementing flexible working hours.

With this new impetus and support for flexitime, Hilles set up a series of task forces to pursue the concept within each of the major operating groups. Each group appointed a work hour area representative whose responsibility it was to put together proposals for implementing a form of flexible working hours. Each of the task forces also consulted with representatives from payroll and compensation as they put together their proposals. The programs were implemented as they were worked out to fit the needs of each individual operating area.

By March or April of 1975, somewhat over 3,000 employees in the Philadelphia area had been covered by some form of flexitime program. These departments included: Personnel, Finance, Administrative Services, Public Relations, Commercial Development, Planning and Operations, Research and Development, Government Affairs, Computer Systems, Sales and Distribution, Marketing, Office Employees in Manufacturing, and Consumer Products. Only two significant groups in the Philadelphia area were not included. The Security Force was excluded because of difficulties in arranging security coverage. Also, production employees in Manufacturing had indicated that they did not want to go onto a flexible working hours program and the Director of Manufacturing felt that it would be too difficult to implement the program. So, traditional work hour arrangements were maintained in Manufacturing Production.

The exception time reporting system used the time recording form shown in Fig. 10-3. This form was merely a device for employees to keep track of their own time. The procedure was based upon the premise that employees can be responsible for their own time and that people will accurately report hours worked. Supervisors have the option, however, to review the time recording forms at whatever level of detail they decide is appropriate for employees in their group. Thus, employees were asked only to report exceptions to the standard work week of thirty-five hours. If no exceptions were reported, employees were paid based upon thirty-five hours of attendance. Exceptions would include overtime, absences for vacation, sick time, etc. When employees did have exceptions, they turned them in on the form to an "exception reporter" in their department who forwarded them to the payroll section; if no form was turned in, employees were paid for thirty-five hours (or whatever the base number of hours were for the particular function or department).

In May 1975, after six months of experience in the larger application of flexitime throughout the Philadelphia operations, SmithKline undertook another evaluation of how the program was going. This evaluation also included a survey of a sample of supervisors and employees as well as a review of operating data.

Again, there was a significant decrease in overtime work, representing an overtime cost reduction of $36,000 or 21 percent between

TIME RECORD

CORE HOURS 9:15 TO 3:00					
DAY	DATE	TIME WORKED		TOTAL HOURS	
		START	STOP	DAILY	CUMULATIVE WEEKLY
M					
T					
W					
T					
F					
S					
S					
WEEKLY HOURS SUMMARY					
REG. HOURS		OVERTIME			TOTAL HOURS
	STR.		1½	2	
Employee Signature			Supervisor Signature for O.T.		
ADVANCE VACATION FROM:			TO:		
ABSENCE REASON					

Fig. 10-3. Exception time reporting form.

the first five months of 1974 and the same period in 1975. Again, SmithKline was careful not to attribute this solely to flexible working hours as there was a general push to reduce overtime, but at the very least the flexitime program did not hinder that process.

With regard to absenteeism, there was a significant decrease in single-day absences among hourly employees during the period of flexitime (early 1975) in comparison with a comparable period in the year before under traditional working hours. Single-day absences were reduced from fifty-one among a sample of one hundred employees to forty-one during the flexitime period. At the same time, there was an increase in total sick days. One would expect that the flexible work hours program would impact primarily on single-day absences, and, even though it is not conclusive that flexitime was responsible for the decrease, at the very least the trend was in the desired direction.

As in the test program in Research and Development, an attitude survey undertaken with a representative sample of supervisors and nonsupervisory employees to evaluate the more broad-scale implementation yielded uniformly positive results. The write-in comments of both supervisory and nonsupervisory personnel were highly enthusiastic about the program. In addition, the survey results suggested that both supervisors and employees perceived a significant increase in productivity as a result of flexitime.

For example, 43 percent of the employees felt that flexible work hours had increased their productivity, 55 percent saw no impact on productivity, and only 2 percent felt there had been a decrease in productivity. Favorable attitudes with regard to the impact on employee morale, the ability to attend to personal business during the day, or on traffic congestion were even more significant. On balance, the survey results represented a highly favorable endorsement for flexible working hours.

There were, of course, some skeptics during the implementation period for the large number of departments during early 1975. However, because of the careful attention provided to the program by Rick Hilles and the task forces which he put together, because of the support from the President of SmithKline, and because the data on results were overwhelmingly positive, skeptics quietly withdrew their objections.

Rick recalls one influential manager who, after about three months' experience in the program, began expressing strong doubts and reservations about flexitime. His concern primarily involved loss of control by supervisors and a feeling that some employees might be taking advantage of the exception time reporting process. Rick reasoned with him, however, saying, "It's taken us a year and a half to test and prove this concept on a pilot basis, and now you've decided after just three months with no hard data that it won't work.

Don't you think it deserves a better test than that?" This particular manager reconsidered his objections and waited for the full six months to evaluate the program. When the data from the questionnaire came in, he was convinced, and the program continued with no problems.

After two years, flexible working hours at SmithKline had become the normal way of doing business. It is a stable way of operating, and there has been no move at all to change it.

Rick Hilles reports a number of observations about flexible working hours.

> One of the most gratifying aspects is how resourceful people can be with regard to scheduling. Employees and supervisors and everyone involved were really very innovative in coming up with alternatives which fit their particular situation.

This resourcefulness in scheduling included such difficult questions as implementing a flexible work hours program in a computer group where coverage was required across several shifts, or designing different programs to fit the workweek requirements for different functions which ranged from thirty-five-hour weeks to forty-hour weeks. But, with a little bit of effort and commitment, all were able to build more flexibility for employees into the working hour arrangements.

The only really significant problem which Rick sees with flexible working hours involves supervision:

> It places much more responsibility on the shoulders of the supervisor for scheduling, for the coordination of tasks, for dealing more directly with employee productivity and working hours. And it's no longer a case where you can rely on the time clock. It has taken some of the crutches away from the supervisors. One caution is that if your supervisory staff has limited skills and experience, then this is going to accentuate some problem areas. Flexible working hours rely very heavily on supervisors for competent management of their people.

But a possible side benefit of the increased responsibility on the part of supervisors is that it forces them to carry out the types of responsibilities they should be doing anyhow in terms of being aware of the job activities of subordinates and being sure that significant programs and projects are adequately manned.

There are a number of lessons which can be learned from this experiment in flexible working hours at SmithKline. First of all, an initial catalyst or advocate was necessary in order to change a traditional system. Rick Hilles and the Personnel Group injected the concept of flexitime into the management system at SmithKline and supported and pushed it to the point where it was eventually successful.

Secondly, the opportunity to test the concept in a benign environment was available: Research and Development. Research and Development traditionally has been looked upon as an environment where employees should be given considerable autonomy. The chances for a flexitime program to be accepted in that environment and to succeed are much greater than in a more structured or traditional departmental setting, and SmithKline was fortunate to be able to test their program there.

Next, data were collected as part of the test and used very effectively in selling management on further extension of the program. The survey results were persuasive, especially the universally positive write-in comments which had high impact.

In addition, the whole program received careful staff attention throughout the test and implementation stage. From the persuasion which was necessary to get the test underway in Research and Development to the extension of the program to the 3,000 persons in the Philadelphia area, the organizational politics were played in a dramatic and successful fashion.

Finally, it was possible to give the program enough time so that the results could be adequately evaluated and so that there could be assurances that all of the objections and potential problems were, in fact, overstated. With enough time, the positive benefits of flexitime proved themselves to the point where, now, it is a way of life in that organization.

Through the flexitime program, SmithKline is reaping the morale and productivity benefits of providing employees with more autonomy regarding their work life, at no cost. They have also moved a step closer toward developing a more open organizational system. And, flexitime is one step in what will probably be a continued evolution of the organizational system.

11
Innovations to Enhance Productivity in Large-Scale Technology Projects

In the evolution of any new industry there are inevitably growing pains. The computer industry has been no exception. From a "standing start" more than thirty years ago, the computer industry has grown over the last few decades into the producer of one of the most powerful tools available for increasing productivity in American commerce and industry—not to mention the entire world. Without computers, our industrial society as we know it today literally would be impossible.

In the process of this general industry growth the design and manufacture of computer "hardware" has also grown in sophistication and complexity. But even more dramatic has been the growth in sophistication and complexity of computer "software"—the programs which control the operations of the machines. And those programs called "operating systems"—the basic heart of the machine which makes it possible for a variety of data processing operations to be performed—are the most complex of all computer programs.

In the early 1970s in the Poughkeepsie, New York laboratories of IBM, some dramatic innovations were adapted to the processes used for creating these very complex, yet critical, programs. These innovations permitted better coordination among the hundreds of programmers employed in writing operating systems; they resulted in significant reduction in errors and increases in productivity; and they charted a path for coping with this dynamic field of ever increasing complexity. In addition, these innovations provided many lessons which can be applied in managing large-scale projects, in general, in order to enhance productivity.

In the early days of the computer industry—perhaps as little as fifteen to twenty years ago—programming was, in large measure, an art. Individual programmers took great pride in the elegance with which they could develop the logic and the techniques for solving the problems which these new machines were so wonderfully able to handle. Programming was an individualized, sophisticated, personalized type of activity, and the individual programmer was often able to handle most of the activities required. The programming code which he wrote was seen as a personal possession which he kept to himself. Typically, the programmer personally punched the code which he wrote into tabulating cards and tested his own programs on the computer, refining the code as needed until it did the job in the way he conceived it should be done. The programmer documented what he had done in a prose format, if at all, so that others could understand his logic and use his program.

Even on projects in which more than one programmer was involved, the program usually was small enough so that the programmers could communicate verbally about how the various segments they were working on should fit together. Cooperative projects in the early days of programming had the flavor of a group of artists, each doing a piece of the total picture using an informal system of communications and liaison to integrate the pieces together.

This worked reasonably well with the early computer operating systems. The number of people that had to be involved was relatively small. And the systems were sufficiently simple, in a relative sense, so that the work of individuals could be integrated into a total system without too much difficulty.

However, as the size of the operating systems grew and the number of functions being coded into the system proliferated, this traditional approach to programming no longer worked. For example, by 1969 IBM was working on an operating system facility which went through a three-year development cycle. This facility—TSO or Time Sharing Option—required roughly one quarter of a million lines of programming code and was developed in four different laboratories scattered geographically across the country. Hundreds of programmers were involved in the development. In an effort of this size, obviously, a great deal of coordination was required.

In 1969, however, the programming community operated, in large measure, with the same philosophy under which it was born.

Each programmer was an artist who did his own thing. The large project was broken up into modules and assigned to individuals or small groups of individuals with the intent of eventually hooking them together into a total system. However, with an extremely large program like TSO it became evident that this approach just was not working any longer.

One of the major problems was that the code which was being integrated into the total system was very uneven in quality. While some of the routines did operate with the elegance and artistic flair with which programmers traditionally liked to pride themselves, other routines suffered either from errors of logic or errors of code execution which did not come to light until the total program was tested—or even later. As a result, very often as the modules to large programs were put together for the test, one bad routine plagued by errors became a "show stopper" which aborted the continued test of the total system until the errors could be corrected. In addition, there were often problems in integrating the various modules when individual programmers exercised their personal style in determining the interfaces between the modules.

Questions of quality became more critical to the customer, as well, when problems surfaced which had not been detected in the internal testing. In programs as large as these operating systems, it is virtually impossible to test every single contingency. As customers put more and more of their applications onto computers, the adverse implication on their business and on their productivity when a system "crashed" because of an error was more and more evident.

By the time of the TSO development cycle, IBM was finding that the question of quality was greatly impacting its costs, as well. The company determined that as much as three-quarters of the cost of producing large-scale operating systems was involved in maintaining and correcting the programs after they were released to customers, rather than in the initial development. It was also very evident to IBM that the cost of correcting a problem increased as the programming cycle progressed. For example, it was calculated that it cost thirty times more to find and fix a problem in programming code after the system had been released to the customer than it did if such problems were found at the point at which the individual programmer wrote the code.

Thus, IBM set out to devise a way to reduce the errors that got into program code initially, to find problems in the code earlier in the development cycle, and to devise ways to improve communications and documentation between the hundreds of programmers who became involved on these large-scale development projects. At the same time, the company was also interested in insuring that programming and support personnel skills were appropriately used in the laboratory.

To respond to these needs, they began to evolve a new way of organizing a large programming effort. It entailed changes in both the structure of the way the programming activity was organized as well as changes in the mechanics of how the programs were written.

Some of these changes were tried in the TSO programming effort. But it was in the development of several of the major components of a program called OS/VS2 (Release 2) (MVS) that these methods were first used all together as a total procedure for program development.

Traditionally, the specifications for a program had been formed in a design shop or project office. These specifications were then "thrown over the wall" to the development shop to be executed. One of the big problems in this was that it was difficult to write down in prose what was in the designer's mind, and the developers often went in a direction which was not originally intended. To counter this, a system of "top-down" design was adopted. Under this procedure, the program is conceived and programming starts by building the total program from the top. It is gradually broken down into meaningfully self-contained subcomponents, and these subcomponents are further broken down in a treelike fashion. As these subcomponents are designed they are programmed and integrated into the total program, so that by the time the lowest level of the program is being written it is an easy matter to integrate it into the total system.

This procedure contrasts sharply with the former technique of programming in which the total design was specified and then programming started on the smallest components, gradually trying to integrate them all at once into a total system. The top-down design, in contrast, is a more evolutionary and continually tested and tuned process.

A new system of coding rules was also adopted to insure that the logic that each programmer used was consistent, easily identifiable, and as simple as possible. This system was called structured programming, and it evolved into an important aspect of programming on large-scale projects and was used as a device for preventing potential errors in the program code.

Structured programming and the top-down methodology deal with the mechanics of how a program is written. IBM also evolved some new methods for organizing the programming activities which dealt more with the people side of writing large-scale programs.

The most significant of these methods was to organize the programming effort into a team. A typical team would consist of a chief programmer or team leader, a backup programmer, and a librarian. The team leader has the responsibility for all of the technical aspects of the project and for the overall design of the program.

This programmer writes the critical pieces of code for the main routines and defines the modules which are to be coded by other team members. He or she is the principal designer of that piece of the program. The backup programmer is an experienced professional who can assume the duties of the chief programmer if necessary. The librarian maintains all of the documentation about the development process and arranges for entry, compilation, and tests for the programs as requested by the team members. Some of the teams also have a system controller who conducts the tests for the programmers directly on the computer. Additional programmers and support personnel are assigned to the teams, as needed, depending upon the stage of the development process.

The top-down design of the program relates to the buildup of the team. As the idea enfolds through the top-down process, members are added to the team to deal with these additional components.

The team organization is designed to do several things. First, it provides for the effective use of senior programming personnel in the team leader and in the backup programmer positions. It also insures that there is the appropriate support for the programmers in getting the job done—the librarian relieves them of many of the administrative chores of documentation, and the system controller carries out their test functions for them. Thus, programming skills can be allocated to actually designing the logic and writing the code, whereas formerly a great deal of time was spent with many of these noncomplex activities.

The team organization also builds a sense of commitment to the project. As one team member comments:

> One intangible advantage of the team approach over other methods of program development is the high level of morale and comradery within the group, even in stress situations—and there are enough of those. The members of the team feel and act as if they are responsible for the success of the whole project, not just for their "piece of the action," and readily assist in areas other than their own to get the job done.

The concept of team organization also gets continuity throughout the development cycle. In addition, it clarifies accountability for problems. Accountability rests with the team leader as he or she is responsible for both the technical design and the development process. The problem of having the project designed in one area and "thrown over the wall" to the developers is eliminated. Under the team concept, as one manager points out, IBM tries to "have the guru who did the design move in and be the team leader for the development. He's usually the first guy placed onto the team."

The team form of organization has permitted a number of practices aimed at achieving quality—getting the bugs out of the program early in the development cycle—as well as obtaining total commitment of the team members to the overall objectives of the project while at the same time insuring that the subcomponents fit together well:

1. There is a formal team leader review early in each project. This is an exchange between the programmers and the team leader to insure that the design is appropriate, that the subunits will work and fit together, and that problems are detected early in the development cycle.
2. Checkpoints are scheduled with the team leader regarding each programmer's piece of the project. The status of each

programmer's team leader review and checkpoints are posted so that all members of the team are aware of them. This provides a picture of the total team's progress on a "plan versus actual" basis so that everyone knows how the overall project is doing.

3. "Walk-throughs" are held with the team leader, the backup programmer, and other pertinent persons. These walk-throughs are held periodically to review the rationale of the project and the detailed code for each individual programmer. At the walk-through meeting the programmer goes through all of the logic of the code which he has been writing. Many errors are detected at that point. These systematic walk-throughs are always done, both on the logic of the design and on the code that has actually been written, before any resources are actually committed to a computer for testing.

The concept of walk-throughs was among the most difficult for IBM to implement. Traditionally, programmers have not liked to share their work as programming has been a very personal art. However, at IBM the rationale for the "walk-through" has been effectively explained to the individual programmers, and the team concept has caused it to become widely accepted.

Walk-throughs are used as a method of error detection, not problem solving. Since management does not sit in on the walk-through, there is no fear of the process being used as an input to performance evaluation. The whole atmosphere is one of a group of peers trying to provide fresh viewpoints and perspectives on the technical problem to insure that all loose ends are covered and errors are detected. When approached with this attitude, walk-throughs have been well accepted by the programmers in IBM.

According to Beth Pilz, a team leader at IBM in Poughkeepsie,

Walk-throughs tie the whole thing together. The design walk-through helps us to be sure that the big ideas are correct, and the logic walk-throughs insure that we don't have to wait until we have a completed project before we look at it.

The results in terms of the quality of the code being written at IBM in Poughkeepsie have been dramatic. For example, the number of problems found in programming code after release to the customer declined steadily after the new procedures were implemented. In one comparison, the rate is about one-third of what it was formerly. In another comparison, IBM points to a reduction by ten times in the number of problems found in new code between two different releases. A major part of such reductions is attributed to the new system for organizing and carrying out programming. There have also been some dramatic increases in productivity. In one comparison, a 70 percent increase in the number of instructions written per man–month is pointed to. The general consensus at IBM in Poughkeepsie is that the new procedures have resulted in dramatic improvements in the quality of code and in the productivity of programmers.

IBM is quick to admit, however, that these measures are not necessarily "clean." They are not based upon carefully controlled experiments, since such experiments are impossible to carry out in large projects such as the ones we have been discussing. A lot of other extraneous factors come into play. For example, it is impossible to separate the positive benefits achieved from structured programming and top-down design from those associated with the team approach, walk-throughs, or better use of skills by having librarians and systems testers on the teams. There is also a component of increased experience among the programmers in the laboratory which results in better quality and greater production. But, on balance, the results are relatively persuasive that there has been significant improvement in quality and in productivity, and each of the components of the new system is credited with at least part of these improvements. As a result, there has been a significant payoff to IBM in the form of increased productivity and reduced costs for maintaining programs after release, as well as significant productivity increases for customers who are less plagued by downtime on their computers.

The concepts employed at IBM are clearly very useful in this large complex technological environment. They are probably not as directly applicable in smaller programming situations. But some of the concepts are generalizable to any kind of project development situation. And, if applied appropriately, they can probably yield productivity and quality returns in a range of situations.

These situations include:

1. Developing an appropriate structure and set of rules to accommodate the project's complexity and insure that there is coordination and communication between the various units and individuals involved in the project.
2. Providing a framework for teamwork and commitment to the project by individual members.
3. Insuring that there is proper utilization of skills: having the appropriate level of support, such as the librarian in the team programming concept, to insure that professionals are not involved in clerical and administrative activities.
4. Providing a vehicle for feedback to project participants about how they are doing and a means for other members of the team to help identify problems which are arising. The walk-through is the prototype.

More recently at IBM, the walk-through concept has been made more rigorous and formal and the process is now known as "inspections." The concept has wide applicability in any situation where the maintenance of high quality is critical; the key difference between the concept as applied at IBM and more typical inspections in an assembly line, for example, is the active participation of the programmer and his or her peers to jointly build as a team an error-free product.

Although these techniques were evolved for a specific program of large-scale program development, they do contain ideas and concepts which can be used in a variety of situations. With increasing complexity in many organizations, there is a growing need for such a systematic approach to organizing large-scale projects.

12
Job Enrichment in a Large Clerical Organization*

The various agencies and bureaus of government often come in for considerable criticism in the popular press when the topics of productivity and efficiency are discussed. Many parts of the government bureaucracy are seen as the epitome of organizations grown almost too large to be managed, of red tape and regulations, or of swarms of clerks shuffling mountains of paper with little identification with and satisfaction from the work.

Whether or not this image is universally valid, there is no doubt that many of the bureaus and agencies of government do employ large numbers of people in jobs that have a relatively limited scope of responsibility—jobs that require little initiative or decision making, that provide little feedback about results, and that yield little sense of achievement or satisfaction. In effect, many of the jobs in large bureaucratic establishments in general—not just the government—offer limited intrinsic motivation for effective performance and productivity. These are precisely the types of jobs for which the concept of job enrichment is supposed to be most applicable.

The techniques of job enrichment are all designed to enhance the quality of work and thus increase worker involvement and motivation. Built on theories about what makes for intrinsically motivating work and job satisfaction, the basic approach is to build on an individual's job so that:

1. The job contains a full module of meaningful work which per-

*Locke, E. A., Sirota, D., and Wolfson, A. D., An experimental case study of the successes and failures of job enrichment in a government agency. *J. Appl. Psychol.* 61(6): 701–711 (Dec. 1976).

forms a clear function with a recognizable beginning and completion phase.

2. The worker has the ability to make decisions and exercise some discretion as to the way in which the work is performed.
3. The worker receives some feedback—preferably from the work itself—about both the quality and quantity of the work which is being produced.

In applying these principles of job enrichment, some of the techniques which are often employed include:

1. Insuring that the worker knows who the user is of the work which he performs—who his or her "client" is.
2. Giving each worker responsibility for a "territory," either in terms of a geographic area for which the individual has responsibility or for a distinct piece of a larger operation or project.
3. Organizing workers into teams so that they can receive feedback and support from their peers, operate toward shared objectives, and balance out task assignments to optimize use of skills and build variety into the work.

In 1973 a major effort was undertaken to try job enrichment within a large clerical work force in one bureau of the Federal Government. This was at the Social Security Administration (SSA), in Baltimore, Maryland. The Social Security Administration employs a large number of clerical personnel who are engaged in work which would be thought of by many as generally routine, repetitive, and with little sense of identity with the work. Based upon theories of work motivation, one would expect many of the jobs in SSA to engender little motivation and commitment for productivity and high work quality and little job satisfaction. The environment would be seen as a "natural" for job enrichment.

The Division of SSA in which the program was undertaken employs approximately 1,000 persons. They are primarily involved in the routine clerical operations of file clerk, typist, mail clerk, examining clerk, and supervisor. The work population is predominantly young, black, female, with a high school education, and doing work at the GS-3 Civil Service classification level.

Before deciding to try a job enrichment experiment, there was a thorough diagnosis of the job attitudes of employees in the division.

First of all, consultants were engaged to hold a series of group interviews in an attempt to uncover the basic feelings which employees had about various aspects of their employment situation. Then, a special 134-item questionnaire was constructed and administered to 516 clerical employees representing four of the major job categories (file clerk, mail clerk, control clerk, and supervisor.)

The survey showed extremely low job satisfaction. Thus, it was concluded based upon very negative feelings about the work itself that job enrichment clearly would be an appropriate technique for enhancing the motivation and satisfaction of employees in the division. Senior management finally agreed with the findings of the survey and eventually gave permission to proceed with a job enrichment study.

Five work groups containing 106 employees were picked as experimental groups in which enrichment was to be conducted. Five matching control groups with 131 employees were also selected. Selection was essentially random. However, due to various work scheduling problems and, in one instance at least, lack of support from middle management, two of the experimental groups never participated in the job enrichment experiment.

The experimental and control groups were:

Group 1: An experimental group which throws, opens, stamps, sorts, and breaks down incoming mail. The control group did comparable work of sorting, breaking down folders to be mailed, putting materials into envelopes, sealing, tying, and loading the mail.

Group 2: An experimental and control group pair in which each conducted searches for lost and misplaced folders, breaking down, and dispatching these folders.

Group 3: A third pair of groups carrying out comparable activities of filing folders, spot-checking for accuracy, and pulling and dispatching folders.

A thorough training program in the theory and technique of job enrichment was undertaken to initiate the project. The trainees included a "key person" designated as the coordinator for job enrichment in the group, the first-line supervisor for each experimental group, one or two employees from each group, an additional management representative, and a union official. The training, which covered three and one-half days, included practice in the techniques of evolving changes to work through brainstorming and problem analysis as well as strategies for implementing the changes.

Following the training, the key person and the other trainees met on a number of occasions over several weeks to decide upon potential changes which could be made in their units. Eventually, in December 1973, the changes were implemented.

In experimental Group 1, the incoming mail unit, processing of incoming mail had originally been done as on an assembly line. Individual employees were assigned to specific self-contained functions in the processing of mail (throw, open, stamp, stamp the folders, place in boxes, etc.). They rotated weekly between the different functions. The output of the unit was recorded by another group to whom the incoming mail was sent after opening and initial processing.

As part of the job enrichment program it was decided that four six-person teams would be set up in this unit. Three of the teams would work on the total sorting function and the fourth team would perform miscellaneous mailroom jobs, on a rotating basis. The three teams that did the sorting were given an equal number of mailbags each day, and team members could decide among themselves how to allocate the various required activities. The teams also kept track of their own productivity and posted the results in the work area.

The work in the second experimental group involved searching for lost and misplaced file folders. Prior to job enrichment, fixed production standards were in place for each job and production records were kept on each employee by control clerks. The supervisor exercised a great deal of control over the work.

After job enrichment, considerably more discretion was permitted in the job, including the decision of where to send finished work (rather than always checking with the supervisor as had been required previously), making calls to other units regarding problem files and keeping one's own time records. Each clerk also kept production records and these were posted anonymously each day.

In the third group, employees put folders in order, filed and spot-checked filing for accuracy, and pulled and dispatched folders. Before job enrichment, employees in the unit had detailed written instructions of what they were to do with special search materials. A control clerk kept detailed production records for each clerk and supervision was very close.

After job enrichment the production standards were eliminated and employees were allowed to decide for themselves, depending upon personal preference and work load, whether to work on initial search or on filing of folders. The clerks also kept track of their own production, which was posted anonymously each day. A rotating position of Unit Captain was instituted with considerable responsibility for overseeing some of the work and compiling unit production records.

The job enrichment changes for the three groups were implemented in December 1973 and the experiment ran for eight months. During the course of the experiment results were measured in terms of absenteeism, turnover, complaints, disciplinary actions, and productivity. In addition, the attitude survey was readministered at the end of the eight-month experiment.

Table 12-1 shows the trends in productivity, absenteeism, turnover, and complaints for the experimental and control groups. In experimental Group 1, productivity increased by 42 percent over the eight-month period. While there was a 17 percent increases in the matched control group as well, this was attributed to the introduction of new equipment and to general pressure for production. The significantly greater productivity increases in the experimental group, however, were attributed to job enrichment. In experimental Group 2—the filing group—production increased by 5 percent. The control group showed a production decrease of 13 percent. In Group 3, because of changes in the productivity measuring system during the course of the experiment, it was really not possible to compare productivity

Table 12-1.   Eight-Month Changes in Productivity, Absences,
Turnover, and Complaints

	GROUP	
	EXPERIMENTAL	CONTROL
Productivity (percent)		
Group 1	+42	+17
Group 2	+5	−13
Groups 1 plus 2*	+23	+2
Absenteeism (percent)	−5	+7
Turnover (percent)	−6	+20
Number of complaints and disciplining actions	0	4

*Data not available for Group 3.

for the experimental and control groups. On the average, for Groups 1 and 2 only where meaningful data could be collected, the experimental units experienced a 23 percent increase in productivity while the control units experienced a 2 percent increase.

As Table 12-1 shows, there was a significant decline in absenteeism in the combined experimental groups, while absenteeism in the control groups increased over the eight-month period. Similarly, turnover decreased in the experimental groups by an average of 6 percent while it increased by 20 percent in the control units over the eight-month period.

The data on complaints and disciplinary actions reported to the Equal Opportunity and Labor Relations Staff during the course of the experiment show two complaints and two disciplinary actions in the control groups and none in the experimental groups. While these numbers are too small to have statistical significance, they are in the direction to complement the results with regard to turnover and absenteeism. At the very least these numbers suggest that there were no negative impacts in terms of complaints and discipline from the job enrichment experiment.

The overall coordinator for the project in SSA points out that the changes in the experimental groups were real and significant. She recalls that the job enrichment changes resulted in less downtime and fuller personnel utilization. Also, by having the group production posted—in the form of a production thermometer of the number of items processed the previous day (anonymously, on a group basis)—employees identified more with the group's productivity. This generated a certain amount of competition to stay ahead of the control groups. In her view, in addition, "The absence and turnover results are good numbers. The employees didn't mind coming to work, because they didn't have anyone standing over their back all day. It was a real live experiment, and I enjoyed seeing the changes."

In view of these combined results, it is generally concluded that the job enrichment did have a beneficial effect on productivity in the three experimental groups. In light of this, however, it is very interesting that there were *no* changes in employee attitudes as measured by comparing the survey results collected before and after the experiment.

To help clarify the somewhat ambiguous results of positive pro-

ductivity effects but no attitude changes, additional group interviews were held about one and one-half months after the formal
end of the experiment. In these interviews, which covered all em-
loyees in each of the three experimental groups, the increases in
productivity were identified as primarily resulting from greater
efficiency and improved work procedures which evolved from
the enrichment changes. The interviews also pointed to a certain
sense of competition in some of the groups which was instrumental
in supporting high levels of productivity.

With regard to attitudes, however, the interviews revealed that
employees were dissatisfied with being asked to do more work without receiving more rewards for their efforts. These employees almost
universally viewed their jobs instrumentally. That is, work was a
means toward making enough money to live, not as a means for intrinsic job satisfaction. When given a choice in the interviews, employees chose a boring job at a higher level of pay in preference to a
more challenging job at the same level of pay they are currently making. Thus, for this group of employees, rewards in the form of pay
and promotion were much more important than the intrinsic challenge
of work. However, the constraints of the pay classification system
in the division precluded such pay increases.

Although there had been no promises prior to the job enrichment
changes that pay rates would be increased as responsibility increased
or as production increased, the employees clearly had come to expect
this. When such increases were not forthcoming, their attitudes about
the work remained at the previous low level.

With regard to the improvements in absenteeism and turnover, the
researchers concluded that there may have been some increased work
interest due to learning new skills and the enthusiasm of being involved in the experiment but that this would wear off eventually as
dissatisfaction over lack of rewards increased.

The results of this experiment, like similar experiments among
relatively repetitive and unskilled occupations, suggest that the
motivational potential of job enrichment may be limited if divorced
from monitary rewards, depending upon the goals and expectations
of the work force. Where workers are operating at a relatively sub-
sistence level, they are preoccupied with the tangible rewards of pay
and advancement and more interesting work will probably have a
relatively limited impact on their motivation unless they are rewarded.

Job enrichment may have a positive impact on production in these situations, however, primarily because it "cleans up" some of the inefficiencies in the flow of work, not necessarily because it impacts worker motivation. To focus more attention on the content of work and build job satisfaction, changes in the work probably will have to be accompanied by increased rewards. When production goes up, people want to be compensated for it, particularly where pay and compensation is the basic motivating factor for an individual.

In the Social Security Administration experiment, it is interesting that immediately after the experiment was concluded the job enrichment changes were completely discontinued in one of the departments. In the other departments, the changes gradually eroded. Part of the problem was that middle management was not supportive of the program. As a matter of fact, middle management had been actively antagonistic to the experiment during its course and had overtly attempted to sabotage it several times. While higher management was committed to try job enrichment and while first-line supervisors felt generally positive about the results, middle management had not been brought in on the planning and had not been sold on the program. This oversight resulted in a great deal of difficulty in implementing the project and also was associated with the eventual demise of the program.

This case suggests that it is possible to increase productivity in a large bureaucratic clerical organization through job enrichment. However, it is quite possible that many of the changes result as much from a better flow of the work and better organization and use of skills as they do from the motivational impact of more challenging work. In environments such as these, it is important to recognize that tangible rewards in the form of increased money and advancement opportunities to compensate for increased responsibility are necessary to increase the satisfaction of the work force.

13
Orthodox Job Enrichment for Changing a Management System*

In the late 1960s and early 1970s a great deal of management attention in American industry was focused on the concept of job enrichment, to the point where it became one of the best known areas of applied behavioral science. There were a number of reasons at that time why organizations of all types and descriptions began to experiment with various ways of enriching jobs.

First of all, job enrichment was seen as a motivational program that was badly needed. It came into prominence during an era in which there was a great deal of talk in America about the declining work ethic, the blue-collar blues, and the eroding productivity of the American work force. Job enrichment held promise for reversing these trends and for directly enhancing productivity by increasing the motivation to work.

❯ Job enrichment was an attractive motivation-enhancement program because it made sense. There is a great deal of intuitive appeal to the notion that motivation can be restored to the work force by restoring individual identity and meaning into jobs which have been made psychologically meaningless by the impersonality of many modern organizations and technology.

The fact that there was a theoretical base for job enrichment—Frederick Herzberg's motivation-hygiene theory—also increased its attractiveness to organizations as a motivation technology. Motivation-hygiene theory, which also has a great deal of intuitive appeal, was

*Herzberg, F. I. and Rafalko, E. A., Efficiency in the military: Cutting costs with orthodox job enrichment. *Personnel*, pp. 38–48 (Nov./Dec. 1975).
Herzberg, F. I., Orthodox job enrichment: A common sense approach to people at work. *Defense Manag. J.*, pp. 21–27 (Apr. 1977).

first articulated in the late 1950s. Job enrichment was a direct technology for applying the concepts from Herzberg's theory. It focused on the core of the "motivator" side of the theory—the work itself—and provided a methodology for differentially enhancing motivators in the work situation as opposed to the "hygiene" elements surrounding the work.

Finally, a significant reason for the meteoric rise of job enrichment as a behavioral technology was the fact that a number of successful demonstration projects were published. Most notably at AT&T and also at other organizations such as ICI, The Travelers Insurance Co., or Bankers Trust, the concepts of job enrichment were found to work and to lead to significant increases in productivity and often in employee satisfaction.

However, by the mid 1970s, a number of organizations were beginning to express some disillusionment with job enrichment. There were reports of instances in which job enrichment programs did not achieve the kinds of positive results which many managers had begun to take for granted. And in some instances, efforts to enrich jobs resulted in considerable disruption to the organizational system, not to mention a great deal of confusion. Whereas some had taken job enrichment as a panacea, more and more managers began to express caution. As a result, some commentators began to point to the "death" of job enrichment, almost taking delight in seeing the latest of the "behavioral science fads" bite the dust.

More reasonable commentators, however, were able to point out why there were serious problems with some so-called job enrichment programs. They attempted to refocus attention on the potential positive benefits to be gained from systematically enhancing the content of work, under the right situations. Some of the reasons given for the problems with job enrichment were that: the concept was misapplied; the concept was applied in areas where there really was not a motivation problem; little, in fact, was done to change the content of work; there was inadequate support for the changes from senior management; the job enrichment became hopelessly intertwined with other activities which focused on things like leadership or organizational climate, to the point where the job enrichment effort became a secondary consideration.

Frederick Herzberg of the University of Utah, who is commonly recognized as the "father" of job enrichment through his early work at AT&T and ICI, pointed out that:

By the early 1970s the whole thing had become a circus. So many people were getting in the act putting their own particular twist to the job enrichment process that in most companies it became a goulash. In Europe, it began to take on ideological overtones. In the United States people talked about enriching jobs, but they lost sight of the basics. Instead of sticking with changing the nature of work they started talking about organization development, leadership, and all kinds of human relations programs which have nothing to do with it. It was, really, a circus.

As the father of job enrichment and as the originator of the motivation-hygiene theory on which job enrichment was built, Frederick Herzberg found these developments to be particularly painful. In late 1973 he was offered the opportunity to assist the Ogden Air Logistics Center in Ogden, Utah in developing a strategy for implementing job enrichment. Herzberg welcomed this opportunity for it gave him the chance to move job enrichment back to the basics where he hoped to demonstrate its effectiveness in a large organizational system.

The Ogden Air Logistics Center (ALC) is responsible for the complete support of a number of the Air Force's key weapon systems. This includes the entire free world arsenal of ICBMs, or the Minuteman and Titan, the F4, which is the Air Force's most widely used aircraft, and a variety of other equipment and munitions. The F-16, the Air Force's newest mainstay fighter aircraft, will also be logistically supported by Ogden ALC. At the ALC, these systems are maintained and overhauled and critical supplies are inventoried.

In the 1972–1973 time period, management at Ogden ALC began searching for ways to increase productivity. In the face of persistent reductions in budget allocations and in personnel, it became more and more important to find new ways of increasing productivity in order to carry out the ALC's vital mission. In addition to productivity improvements by reducing costs and increasing production, at Ogden it was also essential to maintain high levels in the quality of work as there is little room for error in the maintenance of ICBMs or combat fighter aircraft.

Ogden ALC has a work force of somewhat over 18,000 people. The majority (two-thirds) are civilian workers, many unionized, involved in the overhaul, maintenance, and supply functions on the base. The base is Utah's largest employer—larger than the next four largest employers combined—and in 1976 Hill had a payroll of $280 million.

In 1973 the staff at Ogden's Air Logistics Center conducted a comprehensive survey of strategies and techniques being employed to enhance motivation. After investigating a number of possibilities, they determined that job enrichment was probably the most straightforward and pragmatic approach to achieve the kind of results that they saw as necessary to increase productivity and still maintain high quality levels. They contacted Fred Herzberg, who was in residence at the University of Utah, to assist them in developing a strategy for implementing job enrichment at the ALC.

Starting in January, 1974, Herzberg and his assistants undertook a systematic program to orient the ALC Commander and his staff into the basic theory and philosophy of orthodox job enrichment. (The term "orthodox job enrichment," or OJE, was coined to ensure a continual focus on the basic premise of the concept, rather than the "goulash" that Herzberg had seen evolve in many industrial applications.) They placed a great deal of emphasis on making sure that motivator-hygiene theory was well understood and that it formed a single-minded point of focus for the subsequent implementation of OJE efforts. Herzberg was determined that a motivational program implemented at Ogden would not erode into the state of confusion which he saw in many so-called job enrichment efforts being undertaken at that time and which he felt threatened to bring about the eventual demise of the method.

Herzberg's motivation-hygiene theory has been widely publicized and discussed. It appears eminently plausible and simple. Yet, according to Herzberg, it is too often misunderstood, too often wrongly presented, and too often misapplied. The theory holds that there are basically two types of needs which all workers have and both types of needs must be satisfied.

First of all, all workers have what Herzberg has termed "hygiene needs." These needs relate to the environment in which the individual does his job—to such things as the policies of the organization and the ways in which they are administered, supervision, the physical working conditions, the relationships among co-workers, and factors such as money, status, and security. When these factors are unsatisfactory, they will cause the worker to be dissatisfied. However, they do not have an impact on whether or not he will be motivated to produce.

On the other hand, there is another category of needs which operates on a different continuum which Herzberg has termed "motivators." These motivators relate to needs associated with the job itself and when they are fulfilled, high levels of motivation will prevail. They include factors such as achievement, recognition for achievement, advancement, challenging work itself, responsibility, and personal and professional growth.

Herzberg contends that the hygiene needs remove decrements to performance and the motivators lead to improved performance. When hygiene is used to improve performance it does not lead to motivation but to movement and this is short term.*

Orthodox job enrichment rests on a foundation of understanding the distinction between these two different categories of human needs and systematically building more motivators into the job.

The major components of orthodox job enrichment as worked out by Herzberg are:

1. The theory is an essential base which must be employed in all aspects of the program. When managers or key personnel begin to move into areas of the proverbial "goulash" such as leadership theories or communications or interpersonal skills or human relations, Herzberg quickly brings them back to basics and insists that they "focus on the motivators" in the content of the work. Herzberg does not discount the importance of some of these other areas; however, he points out that they deal with hygiene factors—they may make people feel good—but they do not deal with the motivators and thus do little to really enhance motivation.

2. He employs extensive training in the theory and in job enrichment concepts and techniques for all of the key people who are involved. This includes roughly three weeks of intensive training for

*Herzberg, F. I., One more time: How do you motivate employees. *Harvard Bus. Rev.*, Jan.–Feb. 1968.

key persons—equivalent to 120 classroom hours or eight credit hours in a university graduate program. Classroom training is supplemented by considerable practical experience before a key person is considered to be fully proficient.

3. Top management support is essential. Where they initially started with rather passive support from the ALC Commander at Ogden to try some new things in the orthodox job enrichment area, by the time the first pilot project had been completed Major General Edmund A. Rafalko had become a "skeptical believer." Then, as additional projects demonstrated the return to be gained, he evolved into a "skeptical basewide implementor." Since then, most of his skepticism has disappeared. This degree of high-level active support is seen by Herzberg as a vital component for success in any organizational change effort.

4. The "key person" concept is designed to ensure that knowledge and expertise in orthodox job enrichment are available at the operating departmental level, that projects stay on the track as they are implemented, that they stay focused on the "motivators" rather than evolving into a "goulash," and that there are personnel in place to ensure the programs are sustained and tuned to fit the changing needs of the organization. It is a very pragmatic, efficient, and workable system for focusing the attention of a large organizational system onto a strategy for enriching jobs and enhancing motivation.

At Ogden ALC the decision to move ahead with orthodox job enrichment was made in late 1973. Training for key persons commenced in January 1974. Sixteen management personnel were assigned to the three-week training program from each of the center's five directorates. These directorates cover the major functions performed on the base, such as distribution, maintenance, procurement, and materiel management.

Following the three-week training program, the key persons served as internal consultants in their directorates to train personnel in the concepts of orthodox job enrichment and to initiate projects. They worked closely with two groups organized within each directorate. An implementing group consisted of the supervisor of the job which was to be enriched and other supervisors from related areas who would serve as resource personnel. This implementing group determined the actual changes to be made in jobs and how they were to be made.

In addition, there was a coordinating group in each directorate which consisted of middle-level managers. This group served as a review board for the pilot projects which were being implemented. Finally, an executive review group of upper-level managers was also involved to keep abreast of the overall progress of the program and to provide support and encouragement.

In early 1974 the sixteen key persons who had been trained selected eleven pilot projects. These projects covered over 350 direct labor workers such as mechanics, service personnel, administrative and office personnel, and warehousemen.

Each key person served as a catalyst with the implementing group to identify ways in which the target jobs could be enriched. They used a form of brainstorming or "green lighting" to come up with a long list of ideas dealing with possible ways of changing the job. Then, this list was culled to remove any suggestions which dealt with hygiene factors. Some of these "hygiene items" were implemented directly, if they were practical. However, the focus of the group was kept on the motivators which had emerged from the green light sessions. Next, ideas which were clearly impractical or impossible were eliminated. The residue of ideas, then, formed the basis for possible changes in the job to build in more "motivators." The changes were then implemented and the results tracked.

Following three months of preparation and training, eleven pilot projects were implemented over the eight months starting in March 1974. The early projects generally were true experiments in which changes were made in one department and comparable departments did not have any changes made. Then, any available data about productivity and cost effectiveness were evaluated and compared between those departments where the changes were made and the control departments where the changes were not made.

General Rafalko outlined the criteria for the evaluation of the benefits achieved. He instructed his directorates to:

Keep the measurements simple. If you err, err by overestimating the costs of implementing. Be careful in estimating the benefits achieved. Check and recheck your measurements, if you have any question.

The Air Force has an extensive process of auditing costs of its operations, and all of these were brought to bear in evaluating the results of the OJE program. These auditing processes looked at both the costs of the changes and the benefits derived. First of all, functional experts in the directorates evaluated the results. Then, Air Force auditors checked these evaluations and determined that they were accurate. Finally, comptroller analysts on the ALC made an independent assessment of the results achieved.

Actually, this resulted in quite a conservative estimate as only a small percentage of the dollar amounts which were used to evaluate the returns included personnel savings. For example, if one of the projects resulted in a reduction of personnel from ten to six, dollar savings reported may not have included the savings of four employees, since these people would be assigned to another work area. Instead the measurements were based mainly upon the costs of implementing the project—primarily in terms of salary and training for the key personnel—versus the direct results achieved in productivity and cost effectiveness.

A typical pilot project implemented in March 1974, took place in the Avionics Maintenance Section. The Avionics Section is responsible for the testing and repair of all of the navigational equipment being maintained on F4 aircraft. There were three maintenance production lines in the section, and each of these lines was supported by a separate flight test section.

The traditional system was for the maintenance personnel on the production lines to check and repair the nineteen navigational systems on the aircraft. Then, the second group involved with flight test would test the systems and correct any problems which occurred during the test. Only the flight test supervisors had any direct communication with the aircraft test pilots.

In the pilot OJE project, the work flow for one of the three production lines was changed drastically. The functions performed by the production line and the flight test personnel were essentially consolidated. In the test group, mechanics on the production line continued to check and repair various components of the navigational systems. However, rather than turning flight test responsibility over to other personnel, they followed the planes out of the hangar to the flight test. Once they had received training in the test flight process, these mechanics assumed responsibility for correcting any additional problems which showed up during the flight test in the components which they had overhauled. As part of this process, they engaged in direct communications with the test pilots and assumed personal responsibility for the total maintenance job.

Clearly, this was a major reorganization in the jobs for these maintenance personnel. They were given the total responsibility for the maintenance and repair and testing of the avionics components. They had personal accountability. They had direct feedback about whether the maintenance they had performed in fact worked in flight test. And they had a direct client relationship with the test pilots. This enhanced their sense of ownership of a complete and meaningful segment of work.

For the one production line in which the changes were made in 1974, there was a significant reduction in the number of flights required to test the avionics components. During the pilot test phase, which covered forty-seven aircraft, this reduction in the number of flights resulted in an estimated saving of $85,648. At the same time, no changes were registered in the two production lines in which the flow of the work was not reorganized.

Because of these positive results, after the pilot test the other two lines were also reorganized to consolidate production and flight test activity. Comparable savings are now being realized in these lines, as well.

Another pilot project was known as the wing slat project. The work involved fastening a steel strip to the bottom of the wing of the F4 aircraft as part of a modification to improve its maneuverability and provide better stability at high speed. The strap was fastened with 600 fasteners and involved some 217 separate and distinct tasks. Four work crews, each consisting of several shifts, carried out this modification.

One crew was selected for the pilot OJE project. The key person provided the Coordinating and Implementing Committees with training in motivation-hygiene theory and OJE methods. Then, the Implementing Committee applied the techniques to come up with a new way of organizing the work on the wing slat. The crew which originally had had the lowest levels of productivity was selected deliberately as the experimental group for this pilot project.

The OJE changes, which were implemented in April 1974, produced some drastic revisions in the way the work was organized. The 217 separate tasks which formerly had been assigned by the foreman, were consolidated into a single job. This increased the responsibility exercised by the mechanics, heightened their learning, and provided more personal control over the way the job was done.

Also, the two shifts were coordinated so that there was overlap and continuity between them. This provided more personal accountability for the work and direct communications between the two shifts and the possibility for the crews to take more responsibility directly for work scheduling.

Under the old system, the foreman inspected 100 percent of the work. This system was revised so that only some of the aircraft were checked by the foreman. The mechanics did more self-inspection and worked directly with the quality assurance inspectors.

Whereas formerly the foreman scheduled all rework, usually assigning it to a different mechanic than the one who had done the original job, under the OJE changes mechanics inspected their own work and repaired their own mistakes. This gave direct feedback and personal accountability and recognition to the individual mechanics. Formerly, such individual feedback had been missing.

The results were dramatic. While the pilot project group started with relatively low productivity, in comparison with the control group, after a few months it had surpassed the control group in productivity and was the most productive of the four crews. Estimated savings of more than $89,000 were achieved by the end of 1975. There was considerable learning involved in this job; orthodox job enrichment changes seemed to facilitate that learning and to result in significantly more cost effectiveness than the traditional way of organizing.

Several by-products resulted from the wing slat project. One by-product was the significant suggestion for new tooling to make the difficult process of working on the underside of the wing more efficient and less fatiguing for the workers. While such suggestions were not seen as motivators, they were "facilitating hygiene" and accepted as good ideas which evolved from systematically looking at the jobs.

As in the case of the avionics project, the positive results achieved in the pilot project led management to implement the same OJE design concepts into the jobs of the other three production crews.

These are only two of the eleven projects carried out in the initial pilot period. Other projects were conducted in clerical functions, maintenance activities, personnel, a supply and warehouse function, and a computer tape library.

First year results from all eleven pilot projects are summarized in Fig. 13-1.

By November 1974 it was clear to General Rafalko that there was a significant return on investment from the orthodox job enrichment process. The projected annual savings from the eleven projects had totaled over $370,000. It was at this point that General Rafalko moved from being a "skeptical believer" to a "basewide imple-mentor." By the beginning of 1975, the decision was made to "go

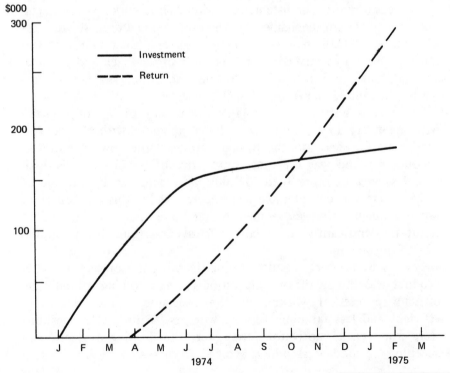

Fig. 13-1. First year: return on investment from orthodox job enrichment pilot projects.

for real." As more and more experience was accumulated, it became clear that there were significant additional savings to be made. Projects covered a range of activities including wing service repair, the plating shop, landing gear door, a total modification program for the F4, instrument repair, and so forth. As General Ralfalko pointed out:

We're going to use this as *the* way of doing work. As we make work flow changes, we will do everything we can to hang motivators on those changes.

By mid 1976, almost eighty projects were active, and a number more had been completed and phased out because of changes in the work requirements. The number was growing steadily, and roughly 25 percent of the base had been directly impacted by orthodox job enrichment in some way. Almost forty key persons were in place and trained; almost 4,000 workers and over 600 managers in almost all of the directorates at the ALC were involved.

Table 13-1 shows the level of OJE activity in mid 1976. For the three years in which the program was in effect, General Rafalko points to $2,700,000 in benefits accruing from the OJE program.

Following the dramatic results demonstrated at the Ogden Air Logistics Center a decision was made to implement the program throughout the entire Air Force Logistics Command (AFLC). A coordinator and staff were appointed by the Command at Wright Patterson Air Force Base in Ohio, several project key persons were trained, and the program has been implemented at the following installations: Headquarters of the Air Force Logistics Command at

Table 13-1. OJE Projects in Mid 1976

FUNCTION	PROJECTS	NUMBER OF KEY PERSONS	WORKERS	MANAGERS
Base Commander	16	6	972	52
Comptroller	7	2	108	66
Distribution	11	4	674	127
Maintenance	13	11	1299	125
Materiel Management	16	9	718	190
Personnel	6	3	45	12
Procurement	5	3	87	30
ALC Total	74	38	3903	602

Dayton, Ohio; Warner-Robins ALC in Georgia; Oklahoma City ALC in Oklahoma; San Antonio ALC in Texas; Sacramento ALC in California; The Air Space Guidance and Meteorology Center in Newark, Ohio; the Military Aircraft Storage and Disposition Center at Davis-Monthan Air Force Base in Arizona; the 2750th Air Base Wing in Dayton, Ohio; and the effort is continuing at Ogden ALC in Utah. The intention is that orthodox job enrichment will become a way of life in the AFLC, potentially impacting some 92,000 employees. In the very short span of just a few years, a handful of pilot projects at Ogden ALC have grown into a large-scale program designed to change the system of management throughout the Air Force Logistics Command. It is probably the most ambitious and extensive program for productivity enhancement through better human resource utilization undertaken anywhere.

It appears that orthodox job enrichment has become institutionalized at Ogden ALC and is on the way to becoming institutionalized throughout the total Air Force Logistics Command. It is true that not all of the pilot projects at Ogden have been rousing successes. But enough of the projects have been successful and the results have been documented in a sufficiently convincing form so that the concept has grown dramatically. Orthodox job enrichment appears to have reached the necessary proportions of a "critical mass" so that there is a reasonable potential for its being sustained, at least at Ogden. By focusing on the work itself and building motivators into the work, the style and structure of the organization is being pushed into a more motivating, more efficient, and more satisfying environment. And by focusing on putting motivators into the work itself, often inefficient work flow and redundant operations are eliminated resulting in greater efficiency as well as heightened levels of employee motivation. Both, greater efficiency and heightened motivation, in the final analysis, can contribute significantly to increased productivity, as demonstrated at Ogden.

In 1977 the Ogden ALC story was still a positive one. It is a rare example of a large system change which seems to be working. There is much to be learned from the Ogden experience about achieving lasting and significant productivity improvements through better utilization of the human resource. The key components of the Ogden experience seem to be:

1. There is a clear frame of reference, both in terms of the theoretical underpinnings for the program and in terms of the techniques of application, which all members of the organization can use as they work to build motivators into jobs. As part of this process, a common language and basis for understanding is built up to enhance communications and to build shared commitment toward the objectives of the program.

2. Extensive training in the theory and in its application is given to key persons to be sure that they understand how the program is to be implemented.

3. Vigorous and active support for the OJE concept on the part of General Rafalko, not just passive toleration, has helped to ensure a running start for the program and a high level of commitment at all levels. Fred Herzberg's very active involvement, as well, was an extremely important catalyst for obtaining positive results.

4. The organization has been seeded with key persons who have been extensively trained and given a charter to "make it happen." They are also given the time.

5. The basic strategy, as explained by Fred Herzberg, was to "go with the winners and then mop up." That is, they were careful to ensure that pilot projects were conducted in areas where there was a good chance of achieving positive results so that success could be demonstrated early. Not that it was a stacked deck—it was not—but some jobs obviously have more potential for dramatic results than others, and those were the jobs that received close attention in the early efforts. Then, once the concept became widely accepted, there was support and encouragement to tackle the tougher more complex areas.

6. At Ogden ALC extensive data were collected on the cost of the program and on the savings realized. Nothing speaks more eloquently to management than expressing what happens in terms of carefully collected and fully authenticated information on dollar savings. Yet the core substance of lasting productivity success is to provide real-life feedback from the work itself which reinforces the six motivational elements.

7. One of the concerns of the OJE program at Ogden was whether or not it would be sustained when high-level support was removed. Obviously, General Rafalko would not be there forever (he received

a new assignment in August 1977) nor would Fred Herzberg be able to devote as much time and attention to OJE as he had in its formative stages. However, there is a good chance that Rafalko's successor will continue active support for the concept as it has now been adopted as commandwide policy. Whoever is the commanding officer at Ogden ALC will have as part of his job responsibilities the active and vigorous support for orthodox job enrichment efforts. Under that situation, there is an increased probability for sustaining the momentum which has clearly been mounted over the first few years of this large system project.

Interim Summary for Chapters 10–13
Illustrating Structural Change Efforts

Chapters 10 through 13 have sampled what we have termed structural changes in the way in which work can be organized. By changing such things as policies regarding working hours, the rules under which work is to be carried out, the system of interpersonal relationships through the formation of teams and the nature of job assignments, performance efficiency and heightened motivation can be fostered. In the four organizations we have just discussed, three different categories of structural changes were undertaken.

In three of the organizations—IBM, the Social Security Administration, and the Ogden ALC—a certain amount of inefficiency was directly removed from the jobs by the changes which were instituted. The new rules for computer programming developed at IBM in terms of top-down design for the program and structured code were simply a more efficient and rational method for completing large-scale projects. The job enrichment work at the Social Security Administration and at the Ogden ALC clearly uncovered many areas of inefficient job design and poorly conceived procedures. When these problems were corrected through the job enrichment changes, an increase in efficiency and productivity was inevitable.

The changes in work procedures and job design in these same three organizations also had positive motivational effects. The whole rationale of job enrichment is to enhance motivation by building more complete responsibility back into the jobs. Job enrichment seems to have been successful in doing this at Ogden ALC and in the Social Security Administration. The team form of organization at IBM in Poughkeepsie undoubtedly also heightened motivation among the programmers with the resulting sense of cooperative effort to produce a quality product, feedback about performance, and openness of information to all team members about the project's status.

The flexitime change at SmithKline was a structural change which increased productivity and employee satisfaction because it removed some of the irritants and impediments to personal satisfaction imposed by unnecessarily rigid company rules. By providing more autonomy and personal choice to employees, the company received a significant return in employee motivation and satisfaction. Whether the flexitime change had a significant impact on productivity is difficult to say from the data available, but at the very least it did not have a harmful impact; the chances are that on balance the productivity results were positive.

This issue of structural changes to enhance productivity emphasizes something which should be obvious but which is often forgotten in the search for exotic techniques for improving productivity: the tremendous potential in many organizations for efficiency and savings by simply cleaning up the work flow. Too often organizations get so immersed in the day-to-day operations that they fail to take a good objective look at just how they are carrying out their operations. Regular attention to this can have sizable productivity benefits.

It is important, however, that this objective look at day-to-day operations not be done as a witch hunt or with the sole intention of cutting staff. If the search for productivity improvement merely nets down to an effort to reduce staff, it will be impossible to obtain the support and commitment of employees. If approached in the spirit of jointly looking for ways to work smarter, not harder, it should be possible to arrive at a number of ways of achieving significant productivity increases through structural changes in the organization and work.

14
Conclusion

These twelve case studies have covered a wide variety of different organizations and different programs designed to enhance productivity. The positive results in each of the experiments have been beneficial to the organizations in the form of significant savings.

In the face of the demonstrated effectiveness of these programs to enhance human resource productivity, it is interesting that in five of the twelve organizations the programs have been discontinued and the situation has reverted back to where it was before the changes were made. In the other seven cases, the changes are still in place, but in several, the prospects for the future appear somewhat shaky.

Why is it that these clearly beneficial programs are not enthusiastically embraced and continued by managements which operate in most areas in a completely rational fashion, highly dedicated to maximizing productivity? What is it about these programs which caused them to fade away in these five organizations? And, in contrast, what are the characteristics of the programs which have remained healthy and vital in the other seven organizations?

In this chapter we shall try to address some of these issues. First we will try to pull out some of the common components of these twelve cases and explain how they fit together into a program for enhancing human resource utilization and quality of working life. Then, we shall try to identify the factors associated with "staying power" and clarify what the factors are which seem to be associated with discontinuance of the programs. Finally, we shall try to outline a strategy for instituting innovations in human resource management which will help to ensure continuing positive returns.

Table 14-1 summarizes the major points of the twelve cases. The

Table 14-1. Summary of the Twelve Case Studies

ORGANIZATION	EMPLOYEES	PROBLEM	CHANGES	RESULTS	LONG TERM STATUS
Supermarket Distribution Center (Detroit, Michigan)	Bakery workers	Absenteeism	A poker game incentive for 5 consecutive on-time attendance days	18.3 percent reduction in absenteeism over sixteen weeks	Program discontinued because of upcoming contract negotiations
Diecasting Company (Midwest)	Forty-three diecasting machine operators	Quality	Regular feedback from foreman about weekly quality and quantity results; positive reinforcement	6.2 percent production increases equivalent to $77,177 annual savings; no change in quality	Discontinued as a formal program when diecasting operation automated; still carried out informally in some departments
Michigan Bell Telephone Company (Detroit, Michigan)	Building maintenance, supplies, and motor vehicle technicians	Low performance on indices of safety, service, and costs	Foremen met weekly to feedback about performance, set goals, and provide positive reinforcement	Over three years, groups went from bottom of the district on performance measures to the top of the district on these same measures	Program continuing, but has not spread to other areas of Michigan Bell
Weyerhaeuser Corporation (Tacoma, Washington)	Treeplanters, truckers, beaver trappers, typists, R & D personnel	Improve production and quality	Various experiments with goal setting, feedback, and schedules of reinforcement	Significant productivity increases in most studies with sizable dollar savings	Research studies continuing some spread through the organization of the concepts
Large Aerospace Company (California)	±30,000 employees engaged in manufacturing electronic components	Quality and production	Participative problem solving, including goal setting, feedback, and training	For twenty-seven projects, 20–30 percent increase in productivity; 30–50 percent improvement in quality	Program discontinued when the production mission was changed

Organization	Employees	Problem	Intervention	Results	Status
The Sanitary Group (New Haven, Connecticut)	Commercial building cleaners	Absenteeism	An incentive bonus for attendance participatively developed by the work crews themselves	6 percent decrease in absenteeism in the participative groups, not in the control groups	Program discontinued due to turnover and lack of middle management support
XYZ Plant of AHM Corporation (New York)	Automobile assembly workers	Grievances, absenteeism, quality	Joint labor/management problem-solving committees	Over five years, 98+ percent reduction in open grievances; 36 percent reduction in absenteeism; 95 percent reduction in body-weld problems; 50 percent reduction in windshield breakage; plus others	Program expanding with continuous positive results
Valspar Corporation (E. Moline, Illinois)	Forty-five total plant employees in paint manufacturing	Poor quality, turnover, absenteeism	Open system of management instituted; employee involvement in decisions: open communications	Turnover reduced by 95 percent over two years; absenteeism by 49 percent; product returns reduced by 90 percent	Efforts continuing to evolve
SmithKline Company (Philadelphia, Pennsylvania)	3,000 employees in Philadelphia area	None in particular	Flexible working hours	Very positive employee attitudes; perceived productivity increases; overtime decreased 21 percent; single-day absences reduced 10 percent	Has become simply standard operating procedure
IBM (Poughkeepsie, New York)	Computer programmers in a development laboratory	Problems in managing complexity of large-scale programming efforts; errors in program logic and code	Systematic rules and procedures implemented; programmers organized into teams; peer review of program quality	Errors in program code reduced by two-thirds; 70 percent increase in programming instruction codes per man-month	Procedures being refined and applied in most large-scale computer programming efforts within IBM and in other organizations

Table 14-1. (Continued)

ORGANIZATION	EMPLOYEES	PROBLEM	CHANGES	RESULTS	LONG TERM STATUS
Social Security Administration (Baltimore, Maryland)	Clerical personnel engaged in mail handling and filing	Extremely low job satisfaction	Job enrichment	23 percent productivity increase; 5 percent reduction in absenteeism; 6 percent reduction in turnover	Discontinued upon completion of pilot test due to lack of middle management support
U.S. Airforce Air Logistics Center (Ogden, Utah)	Craft and office personnel maintaining weapons systems	Need for greater efficiencies and productivity	Orthodox job enrichment	Over eighty projects implemented with documented savings of $2,700,000 over three years	Program continuing at Ogden ALC and being expanded throughout the entire Air Force Logistics Command (92,000 employees)

common components which seem to flow through these twelve cases are:

1. A major factor in enhancing productivity entails simply ensuring that the work is laid out in the most effective fashion, the procedures for doing the job are efficient, proper tooling is available, that workers have the equipment and personnel support that they need to be most efficient, and so forth. In the press toward looking at some of the more exotic aspects of human resource utilization such as behavioral reinforcement or employee participation, we must not lose sight of the large potential gains from simply cleaning up the work flow. Undoubtedly, in several of the cases, at least part of the significant productivity increases resulted from a careful evaluation of the work flow and the design of new procedures. This was clearly the case in many of the job enrichment experiments. At IBM, a new system of computer programming was simply more efficient and supported productivity increases. The joint problem-solving sessions at General Motors, while an example of good participation and cooperation, at the same time often focused on work place factors which were eroding productivity and helped to eliminate them. And the participative program in Spacetronics resulted in many suggestions for an improved flow of work which had markedly positive results, aside from the benefits of participation.

2. A number of the cases demonstrate the potential gains from a systematic program of behavioral reinforcement. These include the processes of goal setting, feedback about results, and rewards for desired behavior. Goal setting is useful in clarifying for the employee what it is that is expected of him or her on the job. It forms a framework for self-evaluation, as well as for evaluation by others. Goal setting is also instrumental in injecting challenge into the job, particularly when goals are difficult but attainable. Ideally, goals should be defined in clear behavioral terms about which there can be little ambiguity concerning when they are or are not met. Feedback—the second behavioral component—is essential for closing the loop on the goal-setting process and providing information about "how am I doing." Feedback is the basis for setting new goals or revising existing goals. To the extent possible, it is desirable to have feedback come directly from the job itself, though in many instances it has to come from supervision.

Finally, the process of rewarding desired behavior is the third important component of behavioral reinforcement. Rewards should be structured so that they are contingent upon the desired behavior; i.e., when the employee comes to work on time, he gets a card in the poker game; if he does not come to work on time he is out of the game. Rewards must also be valued by the employees and fit in with their value system. A poker game incentive was completely appropriate for the bakery workers in Detroit; it would have been quite inappropriate among tree planters in the Bible Belt of North Carolina. Also, rewards should be positive and in all cases maintain the self-esteem of the employee. Punishment or negative sanctions will not reinforce positive commitment to enhance productivity.

The process of building behavioral reinforcement into human resource management should attempt to structure the reward system in such a way that it represents a win/win situation. Returns must not be one-sided, either to the organization or to the employee. Everybody gains from increased productivity.

Also, the processes of goal setting, feedback, and reinforcement can be structured to inject "fun" into the work situation. Variable schedules of reinforcement or games such as the poker incentive may be helpful in doing this. The experiments carried out at Weyerhaeuser clearly demonstrate some of the potential from trying to achieve this.

3. The third common component of many of these cases deals with the extent to which the changes help to increase the employee's personal control over his or her job and work situation. A basic philosophy is reflected which says that workers should be treated as mature adults, not as dependent children or as appendages of machines and equipment. As such, the ideas and opinions of the workers are valid, and they should be permitted as much discretion about how to do the job and how to conduct their relationships with the organization as possible. There should be sharing of information and communication in a spirit of openness and trust and employees should be encouraged to feel a sense of responsibility and ownership with regard to their decisions and their performance on the job. Much of this approach depends upon the style of supervising in the organization, but structural changes such as flexible working hours build upon a similar philosophy.

Direct expression of this type of philosophy is found in the participative management approaches. In the aerospace company which we have described, there was clearly an effort to increase employees' participation in decision making and to solicit employees' ideas as valued suggestions for more effective operations. The XYZ plant of the AHM corporation has a similar orientation, as does Valspar Corporation. This participation and involvement in matters important to the employee was a major thrust of the participatively designed pay plan of the Sanitary Group.

The concept of increasing the employees' control over the work situation is found in a number of efforts to provide employees with more discretion about how a job is to be done or what sort of working conditions are to be provided. Unnecessary constraints are removed as much as possible. Flexitime is a clear example of this increased employee control in a work situation, as is the autonomy to take breaks whenever desired at Valspar, as well as many of the job enrichment innovations at the Ogden Air Logistics Center. By permitting employees more discretion, and by seeing them as responsible adults, their self-esteem is enhanced, their sense of responsibility heightened, and the tendency is to respond with improved work quality and increased productivity.

A related concept entails enriching or building up jobs to be more complete and motivationally meaningful. By asking employees to undertake a complete job with a clearly identifiable beginning, middle, and completion phase—often including quality assurance and problem correction—the employees' sense of responsibility and involvement is heightened. They see that what they do makes a valued contribution, rather than being a small component of some ill-defined larger task. It becomes their job, not a piece of somebody else's job, and they are entrusted with doing it in an effective manner. The usual response is to increase quality and productivity.

4. The concept of teamwork has been found in many instances to be a useful component in improving human resource productivity. Teams can help to ensure that the appropriate levels of skills are available to cooperatively handle various aspects of the work project. Support and reinforcement from peers can often be useful in enhancing motivation and thus productivity. This was clearly the case in the quality improvements in programming code at IBM. Also, in many instances a sense of competition between teams begins to build up

with increased performance efforts and a certain amount of increased fun in doing the job.

5. The final component common to many of these twelve cases is a significant level of management support for the changes. This includes support from senior management in setting a general climate in which experimentation can take place and in protecting it from the inevitable pressures to revert back to more comfortable and familiar ways of operation. In addition, there is an important component of support from middle managers who can sabotage a program of change very effectively, if they want to.

Table 14-2 presents a matrix showing which of the above-mentioned components were brought to bear in each of the twelve case studies. It is evident that in each of the cases there has been more than a single thrust to the change; a lot of things have been going on simultaneously.

Our list of common elements behind these productivity increases has not included several other factors which clearly can be instrumental in enhancing productivity, even though they were not included very directly in these particular cases. The productivity return from the proper selection and placement of employees, from ensuring the right utilization of skills, and from training and developing employees' skills so that they are more effective on the job should not be overlooked. These factors are the old standbys of good human resource management and are obviously very important in fostering productivity.

Table 14-2 also indicates whether or not the experimental program was still in operation and achieving positive results three years following its implementation. In seven of the cases the programs were still operating and achieving positive results. It is probably significant that in all but one of the cases in which the changes lasted for at least three years there was continuing strong management push and support for the experimentation. (The program seems to be continuing at Weyerhaeuser despite the fact that there is no longer the strong management support the experiment received at its outset. At Weyerhaeuser the program is one of a series of research projects; it is not a widespread implementation of the results throughout the company. It is possibly significant that the researcher most responsible for the

Table 14.2. Summary of the Twelve Case Studies

	SPACETRONICS	SANITARY GROUP	XYZ PLANT OF AHM CORPORATION	VALSPAR	BAKERY	DIECAST COMPANY	MICHIGAN BELL	WEYERHAEUSER	SMITHKLINE	IBM	SOCIAL SECURITY ADMINISTRATION	OGDEN, ALC
Work Flow and Layout	X		X							X	X	X
Reinforcement goal setting	X				X	X	X	X		X	X	
feedback reinforcement	X	X	X		X	X	X	X				
Employee Control participation in decision making with management	X	X	X	X								
employee discretion/authority				X					X			X
responsible for whole job	X											X
Team work	X			X						X	X	
Continuing strong management push	X		X	X			X		X	X		X
Program in operation after three years			X	X			X	X	X	X		X

studies is no longer with Weyerhaeuser but is carrying out the research on a consulting arrangement.)

Similarly, in the aerospace industry where there was strong management support for the program it has since been discontinued. Here, severe instability because of an economic downturn and changes in government contracts resulted in a massive reorganization and upheaval in the company. In the face of this situation, even with strong management support, it was just too much to expect the programs to last. As a matter of fact, the supportive senior management was transferred to another location in the process of the upheaval.

Thus, one of the clear indications from Table 14-2 is that strong management support and push on a continuing basis is essential for these types of productivity experiments to be sustained. This means support by management at the top of the organization, as well as at the middle level.

In the five cases in which the experimental programs are no longer in existence, the common theme behind their disappearance seems to be one of change. In the aerospace corporation, as we have outlined, the change in the economy and the change in the mission was just too severe and disruptive for the experiments to be maintained. In the Sanitary Group, the cleaning crews were characterized by high turnover. In those teams where the incentive plan was installed on a participative basis, almost all of the original employees who were involved in the participation had left within eight to ten months. The incentive plan then began to be taken for granted. Employees no longer felt a sense of involvement with the plans. And management, which had not been particularly involved in the design of the programs, gradually discontinued the plans. The changing work force made the participative aspects no longer relevant.

At the supermarket bakery, the program was discontinued because it lacked sufficient management support. There was the fear that the monetary incentive would be subject to negotiation in the upcoming contract negotiations, and management did not want that.

The feedback program at the diecasting operation was phased out as a direct result of changes in technology. When automatic equipment was installed and the number of operators significantly reduced so that there was only a cadre of highly experienced "oldtimers," there was no longer a need for a program of feedback and reinforcement to enhance production. The productivity of the senior operators was already high and this productivity was sustained by the automatic equipment. Thus, the experimental program was no longer relevant to the prevailing situation and it gradually died out.

In the Social Security Administration, the job enrichment efforts had never had strong support from management. As soon as the outside consultants left, management discontinued the programs and the departments reverted back to the way they had been organized previously. Management had just not been thoroughly convinced—at least management at the middle levels had not—and the program had not run long enough to turn them into believers.

These five cases in which the experimental programs are no longer in existence suggest that some "critical mass" must first be reached in order for these programs to be sustained. The existence of a small insular project is extremely threatened unless it has the broad support of management. Even some of the programs which have managed to survive for three years seem to have this type of vulnerability. At Valspar, the climate at the small plant is heavily dependent upon the plant manager. If he is transferred or pressures are brought to bear upon him from above, it is not at all clear that the system can be sustained. The situation is probably similar at Michigan Bell, as the broader corporate environment is not one that necessarily supports the program being undertaken in the Buildings, Supplies, and Motor Equipment Division.

The four remaining cases probably have reasonable prospects for long-term success. The structural changes at SmithKline—flexitime—and the new system of programming at IBM have continuing management support at all levels and are continuing to generate positive results. Flexitime at SmithKline has been essentially institutionalized throughout the Philadelphia operations and will probably be sustained as a normal method of operation.

The two other cases at the XYZ plant of the AHM Corporation and at Hill Air Force Base come close to being large-scale projects with a reasonable chance of long-term success. The changes have begun to permeate the total organization. They have gained support at the top of the organizations and down through middle levels. The employees themselves have felt the positive effects of the changes and are supportive. In effect, the programs have just about reached what might be called a "critical mass" so that they will be self-sustaining in the future. The fact that orthodox job enrichment at the Air Logistics Center has been adopted as a commandwide program provides another level of protection. The prospects for both the AHM process of continuing labor/management cooperation and the Air Force orthodox job enrichment emphasis seem good. And the continuing productivity returns are highly significant.

From these twelve case studies we have derived a number of suggestions for ensuring the success of changes designed to enhance human resource productivity. An organization planning to embark on projects in this area would do well to keep these suggestions in mind.

1. The whole concept of productivity is often a loaded topic for employees and unions. Workers tend to think in the traditional view of labor force productivity as articulated by management in years past. This is the "reduce costs, cut head count" mentality. People are equated to money and easily eliminated with resultant savings. So, when management talks "productivity," unions hear "lost jobs," more often than not. Thus, a guarantee of work is an essential foundation for any efforts to enhance productivity. Productivity gains can only be achieved through cooperative efforts among unions, employees, and management, and full cooperation can only be achieved if job security is not threatened.

2. It is very clear that there has to be strong and continuing support and commitment from management to nurture change programs and let them flourish. Senior management can set the climate and provide the umbrella; middle management must be brought in on the plans and implementation and "own" the programs to ensure that they succeed. Without the support of management, somewhere along the line fledgling change efforts will be sabotaged.

3. Change programs should be installed on a number of fronts simultaneously, rather than as a single insular type of project. While single and narrow changes are ideal from a research point of view to try to assess the effects of clearly identifiable components, the real world does not operate in this fashion. To maximize the chances of success, a shotgun approach rather than a rifle shot should be attempted. This does not mean programs instituted willy-nilly, but it does mean programs which focus on a number of the points of lever-

age for human resource productivity which we have been discussing. There should be efforts to increase the employees' control over their work roles through participation in decision making, greater discretion and authority, and responsibility for whole jobs. At the same time, behavioral reinforcement through programs of goal setting, feedback, and reinforcement can be brought to bear. These programs can also be coupled with concepts of teamwork. Work flow needs to be cleaned up and inefficient procedures eliminated. All of these concepts taken together may be able to move an organization toward more effective human resource utilization and enhanced productivity.

4. Whatever is done should be tailored to the population of employees under consideration and their particular sets of needs. A variable reinforcement schedule with monetary rewards was not appropriate in the Bible Belt of North Carolina; a poker game incentive was highly appropriate among the bakery workers in Detroit or with mountain beaver trappers in Washington State. Peer review of work quality is appropriate with professionals in computer programming; it might not be as appropriate in a production environment, as the well-known conflict between quality control and production departments suggests. Intrinsic feedback may work with research and development scientists, but it does not seem to work with buildings, supplies, and motor vehicle maintenance personnel at Michigan Bell where supervisory feedback is the more appropriate method.

5. In the whole process, a win/win orientation has to be built up. There has to be something in it for everybody. If the organization gets productivity, what do the workers get? The workers may have the quality of their work life improved but there needs to be something more than this, usually something tangible. A gains sharing system can ensure that everybody wins.

6. Change has to reach some "critical mass," or it faces extinction. This means that the change has to be diffused throughout a significant segment of the organization and that the change has to become accepted as essentially a way of life. There is growing recognition of a dictum in this area of quality of working life and productivity change: "Diffuse or die."

Appendix

INTERVIEW QUESTIONS

General Instructions

Try to cover all of the points listed in this worksheet. Record the data and your general impressions as promptly as possible following the field visit. Preferably, dictate a cassette recording immediately. In addition, collect all possible background documentation and data and include with the summary.

To get as broad a perspective as possible, try to consult with a variety of source personnel in the organization. In addition to the individual responsible for the program, talk with senior management, department managers, union representatives, and employees. Try to differentiate inputs from employees who were present when the changes were made from employees coming into the department afterwards.

Type of Organization

What is the organization's major industry, types of products, or services? Are they diversified or single product? What is the organization's history of concern over human resource productivity? What is their industrial relations history? How would you describe the climate (authoritarian, participative, etc.)?

Location

Was the program in a single location or multiple locations? Urban or remote? Are there any characteristics of the surrounding community relevant to quality of work life considerations?

Number and Types of Employees

Number of employees, by major categories (managers, professionals, technicians, operatives). Recent patterns of growth. Skill levels. Any indicators of work force motivation (attitude surveys, turnover rates, absenteeism, grievances, etc.)

THE PROGRAM

What Was Done

Describe in detail all of the changes that were made and the aspects of the organization's operations they were designed to impact. (For example: nature of the work flow (which departments or procedures or processes?); organization structure; reward systems; leadership style; etc.)

To the extent possible, categorize the changes in terms of these categories:

1. Selection and placement
2. Job development and promotion
3. Training and instruction
4. Appraisal and feedback
5. Management by objectives
6. Goal setting
7. Financial compensation
8. Job design
9. Group design
10. Supervisory methods
11. Organizational structure
12. Physical working conditions
13. Work schedule
14. Sociotechnical system

When?

What were the dates of the changes? Were they simultaneous or phased? Was phasing deliberate or random?

Why?

Why were the changes made? (In response to indicated problems; employee or union or management pressure; on urging of a change agent or consultant, etc.?)

Who?

Who was involved in the design and what roles did they play? (management, employees, union representatives, consultants, others.)

How?

How were the changes implemented? (management fiat; collective bargaining; task force or study group recommendations; participant consensus; natural evolution, etc.)

What if any problems were experienced in the implementation stage?

EVALUATION

How were the changes evaluated? What measures were used? Sources of the data? How reliable and valid are they? Was there an evaluation design? What was it?

Who did the evaluation? What skills do they have? Objectivity?

RESULTS

What happened? Record all relevant available data, to the extent possible within each of these time periods:

1. prior to the change
2. six months after the change
3. twelve months after the change
4. eighteen months after the change
5. twenty-four months after the change
6. subsequent

Qualitative (anecdotal) evaluations should also be recorded. What were the key results on . . .

- Production (quantity, quality, costs, other)
- Personnel withdrawal (turnover, absenteeism, tardiness, other)
- Disruptions (accidents, strikes, slowdowns, grievances, alcoholism and drug use, other)
- Attitudes

What accounts for the results? Why does the organization feel they happened? (e.g., skills improved; more ideas generated for dealing with problems; organizational capabilities enhanced; increased zest to do work; clearer goals; greater rewards for effort expended, etc.)

FOLLOW-UP

Were changes made subsequently in the original design? What? Why? When? (Collect the same level of detail as in the "Program" section above.)

In hindsight, what would the organization have done differently? Why?

What is the current status of the program?

Are there plans to extend the program in the organization?

Index

Absenteeism, 5, 9–17, 34, 49, 77, 98, 104, 111, 125, 133, 150–151
Adam, Everett E., Jr., 18
Aerospace industry, 67
Air Force Logistics Command (AFLC), 165–166
American Telephone & Telegraph Co., 155
Attendance, 14, 32, 33
Automobile industry, 88

Baldes, J. J., 41
Bankers Trust Co., 155
Behavioral analysis, 14
Behavioral consequences, 14
Behavioral psychology, 10
Behavioral sciences, 41, 77, 103, 115, 154
Behavioral technology, 17
Bienstock, Penney, 1
Brainstorming, in job enrichment, 149, 160
Burwell, Don, 33, 36, 37, 38, 39

Chaney, Frederick B., 67
Change in technology, 28
Change in tooling, 70
Change, structural, 169–170
Communications, 66, 69, 103
  open, supervisor and employees, 40
Competition, 177
  between groups, 152
  in productivity, 47
Complaints, 150
Consultant, role of, 99
Control groups, in productivity experiments, 3
Coordinating group, in job enrichment, 160, 162
Core period, in flexitime, 119
Cost effectiveness, 16, 30, 34

Costs, 139
Critical mass, in organizational changes, 76, 166, 181, 182, 183
Criticism in feedback, 29

Disciplinary actions, 96, 151
Dossett, D. L., 41
Drucker, Peter, 44

Employee participation, 79, 177
Energy crisis, ix
Executive review, in job enrichment, 160

Faerstein, Paul H., 1
Feedback, xi, xiii, 5, 21, 28, 29, 31, 32, 35, 36, 40, 65, 69, 71, 72, 115, 145, 147, 175, 180
  intrinsic, 36, 183
Flexible working hours, xii, 7, 108, 118–137, 170, 176, 177, 181
Full employment, x
Fun, in the job, 61, 66, 176

Gains-sharing, employee, 107, 111, 113, 116, 183
Gamboa, Victor U., 9
General Foods Corporation, 6, 103
Goals
  difficult but attainable, 31
  difficulty of, 43
  "do your best," 31, 43
  individually set, 68
  set in groups, 68
Goal setting, xi, xiii, 5, 29, 31, 32, 33, 38, 40, 42, 63, 65, 69, 115, 175
  components of effective, 62, 175
  participation in, 43
  theory of, 43, 44
Golembiewski, Robert T., 118

189

Grass roots experiment, 99
Grievances, union, 36, 74, 96, 97

Hackman, J. Richard, 77
Hamner, W. C., 31
Hawthorne Effect, 13
Herzberg, Frederick I., 7, 154, 155, 157, 158, 159, 167, 168
Hill Air Force Base, 7, 17, 181
Hiring, employee involvement in, 103, 107, 109
Hilles, Rick, 118, 123
Human relations, 28
Human resource utilization, x, 2, 8, 62, 166, 171, 183
Hygiene, factors, in motivation, 157, 158, 160, 163

IBM Corporation, 7, 137–145, 169, 173, 175, 177, 179, 181
ICI, 155
Implementing group, in job enrichment, 159, 160, 162
Incentives, 53
    for attendance, 6, 79, 112
    from feedback, 32
    monetary, xii, 13, 20, 43, 54
    poker game for, 5, 9–17
Inflation, ix

Job attitudes, 75
Job challenge, xi
Job design, xi, 7
Job enrichment, xiii, 19, 70, 146–153, 154, 169, 175, 181
    orthodox (OJE), 154–168, 182
Job rotation, 108
Job security, 63

Kagno, Munro S., 118
Katzell, Raymond A., 1
Key person, in job enrichment, 148, 158–159, 160, 165, 167
Kim, J. S., 31
Kinne, S. B., III, 41
Knowledge of results, 31, 43

Labor-management committees, 99
Labor/management relations, 6, 88
Latham, Gary P., 41, 42, 45, 52, 57, 62

Lawler, Edward E., III, 77
Learning effect, 58
Locke, Edwin A., 42, 146
Lost time injuries, 111

Management by objectives (MBO), xi, 31, 44
Matrix organizations, xi
Mech, Robert, 104
Michigan Bell Telephone Company, 5, 32, 66, 172, 178, 179, 181
Mitchell, T. R., 41
Monetary rewards, 53
Morale, of employees, 134
Motivation theory, xi, 71
Motivation-hygiene theory, 154, 157, 162
Motivators, 158, 159, 160, 163
Mountain beaver trappers, studies of, 56–62

National Center for Productivity and Quality of Working Life, xiv
Negotiations, union, 96
New employees, selection of, 103
NIH (Not Invented Here) philosophy, 39
Nunes, Mickey, 78

Ogden Air Logistics Center, 7, 156, 157, 169, 177
Operant conditioning principles, 21, 24, 53, 65
Operating systems, computer, 137
Organization development (O.D.), 89, 99
Organization,
    open system form of, 103–113
    team form of, 169
Organizational changes
    behavioral examples, 4
    humanistic examples, 4, 5, 6
    structural examples, 4, 7
Orthodox job enrichment, 7, 166, 182
Overtime, 124, 132

Participation, employees in problem solving and decision making, xii, xiii, 44, 66, 67, 68, 69, 87, 104, 115, 145, 175, 177
Participation in goal setting, 31
Payments, balance of, ix
Pedalino, Ed, 9, 10, 11, 14, 16
Peer review, of work quality, 183
Performance appraisal, 29
Performance measurement, 69

Planning, business, 31
Praise, 33
Problem solving, 115
  employee participation in, 91–92
  joint, labor/management, 6, 88–102
Peter Principle, 83–84
Production, goals of, 69
Production costs, 70
Productivity
  capital, as a factor in, x
  criteria of change in, 3
  customer dissatisfaction, as a factor in, 19
  inputs to, ix, 1
  organizational disruption, as factors in,
    xiii
  outputs from, x, 1
  personnel withdrawal, as a factor in, xiii
  production, as a factor in, xiii
  ratio concept, ix
  re-work, as a factor in, 19, 20
  scrap, as a factor in, 19
  technology, x
  work quality, as a factor in, 18
Productivity criteria
  costs, 33
  safety, 33
  service, 33
Programming, computer, 141
Programming, structured, computer, 141,
  144
Project teams, xi
Pursell, E. D., 42

Quality
  goals of, 70
  product, 70, 105, 110, 139, 144
Quality assurance, 73, 177
Quality control, 18, 19
Quality of working life (QWL), xiii, 2, 6, 8,
  87, 93, 94, 97, 100, 103, 104, 106, 117,
  131, 171, 183

Rafalko, Maj. Gen. Edmund A., 154, 159,
  160, 164, 165, 167, 168
Rate buster, x
Reinforcement, xii, xiii, 63, 65, 175–176
  behavioral, 63, 175, 176
  continuous schedule of, 54, 57, 63
  extrinsic, 65
  intrinsic, 65

  operant, 42
  positive, 5, 29, 31–40
  schedules of, 5, 53, 56, 57, 58, 115
  variable schedules of, 5, 54, 57, 63, 176,
    183
Reparticipation, employee, 86, 87
Rewards, monetary, 152
Re-work, 70
Role playing, 35

Safety, 34
The Sanitary Group, 6, 77–86, 115, 116,
  173, 177, 179, 180
Scheflen, Kenneth C., 77
Scientists and engineers, goal setting for, 5,
  50–51
Selection and placement, 178
Sensitivity training, 78–79
Service, quality of, 34
Sirota, David, 146
Skill utilization, xi
Skinner, B. F., 42, 53
Smithkline Corporation, 7, 118–136, 170,
  173, 181
Structured code, in computer programming,
  169
Support
  management, 178
  middle-management, 116
  senior management, 116

Team leader, 141, 142, 143
Team leader review, of project, 142
Teams, 7, 147, 177
  autonomous, 103
  of computer programmers, 141, 144
Teamwork, xiii, 177
Technology, changes in, 27
Teel, Kenneth S., 67
Time clocks, 108, 122, 124
Time sharing option (TSO), 138
Theory Y, 78, 84
Top-down design, in computer program-
  ming, 140, 144, 169
Traditional model presentation, 106, 107
Training, job, 178
The Travelers Insurance Company, 155
Tree planter, studies of, 54–56
Trust, climate of, 106, 107, 108, 116
Turnover, employee, 87, 104, 111, 150, 151

Union contract negotiations, 14
Unions, international, 100
U.S. Airforce Air Logistics Center, 174
U.S. Bureau of Labor Statistics, 77
U.S. Social Security Administration, study
    in, 7, 146–153, 169, 174, 179, 181
Utilization of skills, 178

Valspar Corporation, 6, 104–113, 115, 116,
    172, 177, 179, 181
Values, of the employee group, 26

Wage-hour laws, 120
Walk-throughs, in computer programming,
    143, 144

Walsh-Healy Act, 120
Weyerhaeuser Company, studies in, 5, 42–
    64, 172, 176, 178, 179, 180
Win/win, orientation, 176, 183
Wolfson, Alan D., 146
Word processing, 49
Work in America Institute, Inc., xiv, 1
Work-related discipline, 96
Wright Patterson Air Force Base, 165
Wurtele, C. Angus, 104

Yukl, G. A., 41, 42

Zero defects programs, 19, 21